Beyond

The

Threshold

Simple Transformational Techniques to

Awaken Your Potential

Dean Nelson

Seven Cardinal Gates

Publishing

Seven Cardinal Gates
Publishing

Acknowledgements

Thank you, Dr. Joe Vitale, for your endorsement of my book. I truly appreciate all you do to enlighten and inspire people to create positive change in our world.

Many thanks to my editor, Michelle Schacht, for her outstanding work. She encouraged, motivated, and inspired me to dig deeper and create more meaningful passages. Visit her at wordofmouthediting.com.

I am extremely grateful for all my proof-readers and the feedback they provided: Paula Nelson, Mike Bedenbaugh Jr., Susan Raible, Van Nelson, and David Price.

Thank you, Stephenne Garcia, for your invaluable assistance with the launch and promotion of my book.

3

Table of Contents

Chapter One

Short-Cuts to Long-Term Change

Transformation Made Easy

I've got good news and bad news. I'll give you the bad first.

Bad News: You only have one life to live.

I actually see that as good news, however, it's bad in the sense that if you don't live it right, to the best of your abilities, you don't get a second chance at it. Every day, hour, minute, and second that passes us by is gone forever. We don't own time and we can't stop time. If you take a three-hour nap, you can't get that time back. You can try. You can tell yourself, "No, no, wait. I meant to take a fifteen minute power nap. I overslept. I need most of those three hours back, please." But you're not going to get it back.

Some people say we live many lives, and that may be a possibility. If that is true, we can't take anything we may have learned from a previous life into the one we're currently living. So regardless of how you look at it, you only have one life to live. If you don't live it right, that's bad news.

Good News: You control your life.

You might feel stuck in one or many areas of your life. You might not be happy in your marriage or romantic relationship. You may not like your job, some co-workers you're forced to spend time with, or your pay. You might feel handicapped in some way because of your family lineage, your gender, your race, your weight, your education, your height, your looks, or your age.

You might feel as if many decisions in life are made for you, not by you. For example, you may not have had enough money to buy a new car, so you bought what you could afford, not what you would like to drive. Not being able to make decisions has probably made you feel helpless, like an unmanned canoe at the mercy of a river's strong current.

Each one of us is in desperate pursuit of whatever happiness means to us, be it money, a particular person to marry, a noble legacy to leave, properties, peace in our homes, to be respected, or to be loved. In doing so, we live on a planet with billions of people doing the same thing, frequently bumping into one another like unmanned canoes in the river of life, many of us lost and feeling as if the current decides, not us.

If at times you feel like this, you're not alone. But that's ok, and I'll share with you why.

I'm going to share with you how to take control of your life and to live it by your design.

For starters, I can tell you have a desire to change for the better. Hence, you're reading this chapter… probably wondering if you should read more. I suggest you do. In this book, I'm going to show you some shortcuts to long-term change.

Historically, the main problem people have with changing is that it takes too long. It takes too long to lose thirty pounds; that requires going to the gym or working out three times a week for months, foregoing the greasy, butter-rich foods we love, and eating healthy for months. It takes too long to learn to play the piano; that requires hours upon hours of practicing, starting with just one finger, then being able to use your two pointer-fingers, then maybe take lessons… who has time for that?

Imagine if you could lose those thirty pounds in two weeks or if you could play piano with both hands, eyes closed, to a room full of awed listeners in a month. In a sense, that's what I'm going to provide you with – shortcuts to long-term change!

It is possible to convert mundane, everyday life into meaningful, joyous expressions of ourselves. But we don't discover new places by following established paths.

I can only provide you the information but I can't change you for you. However, you can. You control your life. If you can manifest into action what you're going to learn in this book, I guarantee you, you're going to live a better, happier, and more fulfilled life.

You know you were meant for more than you're doing, more than you're making, more than you're laughing, more than you're loving, more than you're living… you just haven't found out exactly how to get there. It's frustrating, I know. I've lived this too!

I would love to live in a world where every inhabitant was a little nicer, a little more pleasant, a little more tolerant, a little more understanding, and a little more forgiving. Wouldn't it be great to live in a world where the whole of humanity didn't settle for average?

If we could all participate and get better, even minimally, we would enhance our civilization, treat our planet better, and enrich the future lives of our children. Changing the world starts with helping change one person. That person just may be you.

I want you to know this important truth - the path to self-development does not have to be walked alone.

I'm here to help, as are many others already in your life and ones you haven't met yet.

Open your mind, be honest with yourself, and take advantage of the time you invest in reading this book. There's a strong wind of change coming: a wind strong enough to fight life's currents. You may have tried, unsuccessfully, over and over again to change. If so, I'm happy for you that you haven't given up because I have one more bit of good news – living a happier and more positive life is not as difficult as it seems. Welcome to the beginning of your transformation.

How To Read This Book

In the following chapters, we will delve into topics that tie into crossing the threshold of higher consciousness. I have chosen subjects that are crucial to our ability to thrive in and adapt to the world we live in today.

But it's not just about reading. Success demands applying what you've learned. So, at the end of each chapter, you will find sections entitled "Solutions" and "Resources" covering various challenges ranging from personal to business issues.

In the Solutions section, I present action steps for handling life challenging issues in a way that brings about positive transformation to a happier way of living. By no means are these solutions the only avenues to pursue; they are to open your mind and get you started.

You will also find in the Resources section helpful suggested sources that provide additional, relevant information should you wish to delve into the chapter topic further. They have been invaluable to me in preparing this book for you. In addition, all of the links in the Resources section can be found on my website, www.awakenmypotential.com. You will find the information listed in order by chapters.

Feel free to read this book selectively. It's okay to skip around chapters depending on what you need to transform in your life first. Also, do not think you have to implement every action or explore every resource at once. To bring about the change you want, you may find it more effective if you digest what I suggest in small servings. You might want to spread out this book over a specified timespan. This will enable you to figure out what works best for you.

Now, go get started on your journey!

Chapter Two

Awakening Potential

How To Master Your Unrealized Potential

I consider myself to be somewhat of a self-improvement enthusiast. For more than thirty years, I have devoted myself to life improvement. My sincerest endeavor in writing this book is to share some essential life-changing philosophies and processes with those who are interested in learning about and growing their potential. The tools and techniques I am about to share have helped me and I trust they will help you.

Not everyone is interested in improving their lives. Many are happy with their life just as it is, and that is perfectly fine. Some people believe it is too difficult to make lasting, meaningful changes. They resist opportunities to develop themselves mentally, emotionally, or spiritually. Even physical improvement can be a challenge for many people. They get discouraged with diets and exercise when they do not achieve positive results quickly enough.

(By the way, I don't think you belong in these groups because you're already improving yourself by reading this book.)

Can you imagine how the coach of a professional sport or Olympic team feels when one of his players is not performing to his or her potential? The job of the coach is to bring out the very best in their team. That's my attitude for writing this book for you, and in my daily interactions with those around me who are interested in learning from my experiences.

If you think of those you know, the drive system of each individual varies greatly. Some are content with whatever comes their way, and others are driven to succeed and excel in many areas of life.

Our world needs everyone to participate at whatever level they choose. We need those who are *not* driven to financial success, those who do *not* have high IQ scores, those who are *not* physically strong, those who possess little or no ambition, and so on. The planet has needs for housekeepers, truck drivers, physicists, garbage collectors, doctors, laborers of all sorts, teachers, salespeople, psychologists, farmers, and welders. You get the idea.

Everyone cannot be a Nobel Prize winner or an electrical engineer. Each of us serves humanity in specific ways. What would life be like if our world was only comprised of high-powered executives or politicians?

Our civilization develops and improves as we each contribute in our unique ways. It takes all of us working together to nurture our planet.

Anyone can reach a higher level of potential in an area of life at any time. If we cannot lose weight or build muscle, we can at least strengthen our muscles and attain a healthier state at our current weight. If not satisfied with our education level, we can enroll in educational courses at a school or online. If not emotionally happy, we can seek therapy, read books, and explore other ways to improve our emotional state. If not content with our spiritual lives, we can delve into the spiritual world through whatever means we wish.

Even if we do not reach our greatest potential, and have no aspirations to ever do so, we can improve any area of life as minimally or extensively as we want. Surely, there is one small thing that each of us has a desire to improve upon. It may only be socially or work-related, but opportunities to improve are always available.

Why should we consider expanding our potential? Because the entire human race depends on those who have dedicated their lives to reaching beyond average.

What if scientists did not push forward with extensive research for cures of diseases? Competitive sports would be boring if athletes did not excel in performing to the very best of their abilities. What would we know of our universe if physicists and cosmologists did not thrust themselves into the unknown with determination and zeal?

Awakening our potential is supremely vital to the survival of our planet. It is the spirit of humankind to endeavor into the possibilities of expansion and development of our civilization.

The very survival of the human race depends on those who are willing to resist mediocrity and aspire for greatness. It does not mean all of us have to achieve monumental success in business or acquire great wealth. It only means if each of us pushes just a bit more to bring out the best in ourselves, then we have a better chance of making the world a finer place for our children and for those who follow.

Awakenings of potential can happen on small or grand scales. We can experience a multitude of these awakenings during our lifetime. When we remain open-minded and self-aware, we can attract opportunities to develop ourselves in ways we may not have otherwise considered.

Just the act of bringing self-improvement to mind often can bring about circumstances that will be conducive to awakening your potential.

If you are serious about making the most of your life and creating more excitement with your experience, then consider the following suggestions.

Solutions

- *Set a goal to improve on something.* Goals create excitement and, when achieved, they generate feelings of satisfaction and accomplishment. Merely the process alone of engaging with goals engenders enthusiasm.

- *Acknowledge that unrealized potential can leave you feeling unfulfilled in some ways.* It is like paying for a seven-course meal and only receiving five.

- In order to discover areas for improvement, ask yourself questions like, "What can I improve in my life?" and "How can I go about being the very best at _____?" Or, "What would I do and could I do to improve something about me today? How would I reward myself?"

- *Be real about it.* Remember, what you aim at determines what you will see. If you set a goal to meet positive people, you will notice more positive people around you.

- Conduct research on the area(s) you wish to improve upon. View websites and read papers on your field of interest. Discover what others have done to become leaders or top performers in their industry.

Tony Robbins, the popular speaker and motivator, offers the following suggestions based on his book, *Awaken The Giant Within.*

- *Focus on what you want to believe.* "Our life experience is based on what we focus on," Robbins says. "You [can] focus on things that haven't happened yet, and feel good about them in advance."

- *Create a mental evidence manual.* "Think of your past 'wins' and successes to help motivate you to future ones. Think of a time when someone complimented you on your looks or on your abilities. Think of a time when you completed a project that you were proud of." (I try to reflect on times when I made the very best choices.)

- *If you don't like your story, create a new one.* "People can succeed if they imagine something vividly enough just as easily as if they had the actual experiences." Affirmations can be a powerful tool to reinforce a belief. An affirmation is a statement that you write down and then repeat in your mind frequently. Don't just repeat these statements perfunctorily, vividly imagine them often.

- *Establish certainty.* Your thoughts continuously influence what you believe. Developing assurance strengthens your beliefs and may prevent you from losing confidence. An attitude of certainty may help you accomplish more of your goals and dreams. (I monitor my self-talk and constantly shift my attitude toward confidence.)

- *Utilize fear as a motivator.* "Make the pain of not changing feel so real to you, so intense, so immediate that you can't put off taking that action any longer," Robbins recommends.

- *Decide on your own identity.* "One of the strongest forces in the human personality is the drive to preserve the integrity of our own identity. Your identity is nothing but the decisions you've made about who you are, what you've decided to fuse yourself with."

- *Reward yourself for your successes.* Robbins advises that you "set up a series of short-term goals or milestones, and as you reach one, immediately reward yourself." This is a great motivator to continue on your path.

- *Get your blood moving.* "Your state of mind affects your performance and moving your body is a great way to influence your state of mind." Getting in shape will improve your physical condition, which will change the way you view your circumstances.

- *Develop an optimistic vocabulary.* "Simply by changing your habitual vocabulary — the words you consistently use to describe the emotions of your life — you can instantaneously change how you think, how you feel, and how you live." (I like to replace disabling phrases like "I always forget to listen more to others" with "I am constantly improving my listening skills.")

Resources

Psychology Today: www.psychologytoday.com. Search for the article "The After-Effects of Awakening."

HealthnFitness: www.healthnfitness.net. Search for the article "7 Things That Happen To Your Mind and Body When You Start Meditating."

The Magic Happens Magazine: www.themagichappensnow.com. Search for the article "Awakening Potential."

The Chopra Center: www.chopra.com. Search for the article "Awaken Your Creative Response."

Reminder: You can find all live resource links on the author's website at AwakenMyPotential.com.

Chapter Three

A Life-Altering Experience

I Know Whereof I Speak

At the impressionable age of fifteen, I was flipping through the pages of my life trying to discover myself. I was unsure of who I was and wondered why life seemed so difficult and challenging. I was no different than any other teenager until that horrifying moment.

Family life appeared to me to be stable and normal. I know my parents had suffered a major relational issue that had created a lot of tension between them. But the problem looked to be resolved and life, in my eyes, was returning to a state of normalcy.

Then, without notice, on the Sunday before my first day of high school, my normal life came to an end. My mother came to me and told me my father had placed his shotgun in their shower. My older brother was not home and I told her I would call for help.

I was frightened and unsure of how to handle the situation. I had no idea of my father's intentions. I did not want to use the phone in our home because I did not want my father to hear, so I ran a half mile to the shopping plaza to use a pay phone. (Cell phones didn't exist at the time.)

I decided to call a family friend, Delores. In my nervousness, I inadvertently dialed the police department and promptly hung up the phone upon realizing my mistake. I only had one quarter for a single phone call, so I ran across the street to a gas station and asked to use their phone. I reached Delores and she came over immediately, arriving at our house before I returned. She took my mom to our next door neighbors.

I entered our house and made my way to my parents' bedroom door. I called out, "Dad, Dad," but there was no response. The door was locked, so I reached for the key stored above the door on the ledge of the doorframe. At the moment my hand felt the key, a blast from his shotgun rung out. I called again to him, but no reply came.

Then, I ran outside of the house to my parents' bathroom window. It thankfully was open. I eased my way near the window and called out to my dad once more. No response.

I dashed back in toward their bedroom door. BAM! Another blast of the shotgun broke the air as I stopped at their door. My entire body was shaking in extreme fear. Somehow, I mustered up the courage to unlock the door with my excessively trembling hands. The room was layered with gun smoke and there was a deafening silence in the room. I noticed a large hole in their dresser that the first shot had created.

Slowly and cautiously, I entered the bedroom. I made my way to the open bathroom door. There laid my father in the shower with a hole in his chest and blood splattered everywhere. The horror of the sight was compounded by the sound of blood oozing from his veins.

This terrifying experience left me emotionally wounded for many years to come. I suffered from intense guilt and shame. I formed many damaging beliefs as a result of that incidence. Beliefs like, "It is my fault he is dead for not telling the police while I had them on the phone; I am to blame for not getting him to speak with me; I am a bad son; I let my family down; I am a failure," and many other harmful beliefs as well.

I share this story with graphic details so you can understand the enormous impact this event had on my life. I became depressed and suicidal. Those tragic memories haunted me for many years. My recovery was long and slow.

At about age twenty-five, my quest for emotional healing and closure began. As a result of the stress of living with such guilt and shame, I had developed a severe and debilitating case of ulcerative colitis, a disease of the colon.

I came to understand that the power of my beliefs had influenced all of my life's decisions and choices.

Unfortunately, it influenced them negatively! This impacted my life in so many ways that I had become ill and was miserable.

I began reading books, purchasing audio and video programs, researching various therapies, and attending self-improvement and life enrichment seminars. I was obsessed with self-development because I needed to advance beyond this horrifying event.

I later discovered ways of eliminating these harmful beliefs, creating new, positive beliefs to replace them. I present in this book the resources that helped me to effect massive changes in my life and have brought me to a place of good health, peace, happiness, and a sense of fulfillment.

This is my wish for you.

Solutions

• Set aside time each day for meditation. These sessions of mental quietness are a powerful way of structuring a break from data absorption and pro-mote psychological and physical rest. Take this time in solitude just for you. Schedule time for yourself daily in stillness.

• Understand the importance of beliefs and how they impact your life and direct your path. Read chapter eleven to learn how to eliminate negative beliefs and to create new empowering beliefs.

• Be tenacious about moving beyond your past ad-verse experiences. Practice new ways of overcom-ing obstacles and changing negative behavior pat-terns with the solutions, resources, and exercises presented in this book.

• Monitor your memory. Observe the times when you get caught up in reliving your past. Choose to refrain from dredging up old, negative memories of past failures or perceived incompetency.

• Even if you feel that your life has been shattered by dreadful events, know that you can be shattered and still be whole. Consider a windshield of a car that was hit by an errant golf ball. It may be shat-tered but, it is still whole.

Resources

American Psychological Association: www.apa.org. Search for the article "How to Cope When a Friend or Loved One Dies by Suicide."

Psychology Today: www.psychologytoday.com. Search for the article "Understanding Survivors of Suicide Loss."

Jon Kabat-Zinn, Ph.D.: www.mindfulnesscds.com and Sounds True: www.soundstrue.com. Each site offers mindfulness and meditation CDs and information. Also, check out Jon's books: *Full Catastrophe Living; Wherever You Go, There You Are;* and *Mindfulness for Beginners.*

Tom Cronin: www.tomcronin.com. Mindfulness and meditation techniques.

AwakenMyPotential.com: www.awakenmypotential.-
com. Read my short book "The Experiential Approach" to learn more specifics about how I overcame
the death of my father.

Laura Silva Quesada: www.laurasilvaquesada.com.
The Silva Method for Meditation.

**Reminder: You can find all live resource links on
the author's website at AwakenMyPotential.com.**

Chapter Four

The Technology Dilemma

How Technology Can Disconnect Us

Have you noticed so many of us have become numb to the subtle urges of our higher selves? If you were to ask a friend or even someone in the street to describe their daily connection to a power greater than themselves, you'll likely be greeted by a blank stare and a noticeable pause before the person could articulate his answer.

Where is this disconnection coming from? I believe it's because we are so absorbed in our jobs and personal relationships that we have neglected the impulses of our divine natures. We seek to indulge ourselves in the immediate pleasures of achieving success or placating those surrounding us in our personal and business domains rather than look outside our microcosm to a bigger view.

Our attention pivots on an exaggerated sense of accomplishment and a constant urge to multitask a wide array of daily activities. We drive ourselves to complete more tasks than we are capable of in a day while wondering why our energy levels are depleted.

At the end of the day, so many need to turn to an external source of relief. We find ourselves seeking solace in adult beverages, an evening of television, an overindulgence of food, a marathon video game, or the impulsive activity of social media.

How has this degradation of life come about?

It's happened, in part, by the prevalence of technology and our being glued to a screen. I do not see the world's increasing implementation and reliance on the beneficial aspects of technology as a decline of society. Technology has made our world a better place in innumerable ways. I am not, by any means, denouncing it. It serves us well.

Rather than seeing decline, I view technology as an agent of transition. Our world culture has indeed transitioned into a technologically evolved society. Every area of life has been impacted by these advances.

Mainstream society readily accepts the use, or over-use, of technology as a means to navigate our way through daily activities. However, when we become obsessively dependent on technology to such a degree that our lives become disconnected from ourselves and other people, it does more harm than good.

Have you noticed in the coffee shops how many people have their eyes glued to a screen rather than in exploring conversation with another? When we become burdened by the countless technology-dependent ways we interact with our environment and those surrounding us, often in a mechanical, detached manner, then it impedes our personal performance.

Technology can be distracting at times and disable many of us from completing tasks in a timely, proficient manner. These distractions can dilute our efforts and divide our minds to the point of mental exhaustion.

In a New York Times article titled "Gray Matter" by Bob Sullivan and Hugh Thompson, they asked Alessandro Acquisti, a professor of information technology, and Eyal Peer, the psychologist at Carnegie Mellon University to design an experiment to measure the brain power lost when someone is interrupted.

The experiment consisted of 136 subjects who were asked to read a short passage and answer questions regarding the reading. During multiple tests, the participants were interrupted twice, and the results were astonishing.

The study found that the distraction of interruptions combined with the drain of preparing for those interruptions made the subjects 20 percent "dumber," which correlates to a B-minus student dropping into a failing score.

In another article by NBC News columnist, Bob Sullivan (2013), he speaks of "depressing" research by Gloria Mark at the University of California, Irvine. Mark says that typical office workers only get eleven continuous minutes to work on a task before a smartphone interruption occurs.

Sullivan also explains that neuroscientists refer to multitasking as "rapid toggling" between tasks as the brain focuses quickly on one topic, then switches to another, and another. "As all economics students know, switching is not free. It involves 'switching costs'—in this case, the time it takes to re-immerse your mind on one topic or another."

An example would be a worker compiling data for a detailed report. Each time he is interrupted by a text, email, or alert on his smartphone, he is distracted and loses his place on the report. He has to take a moment to remember where he left off. This can lead to omissions and errors.

How sad that the use of technology is interfering with our educational system in ways that were not properly assessed before its implementation. Technology was initially determined to be a learning tool that would support our schools and universities. Actually, it is doing just the opposite of that.

The problem is that people—students and adults—are not taught how to use technology to benefit and reinforce our educational system and our personal lives. We do not fully understand how to cope with the rapid advances in technology and how to use it wisely and responsibly. There doesn't exist any wide-spread training on this topic, if there even exists a set training.

One study by Professor Rosen of California State University, Dominquez Hills (2011), mentions how technological distractions of smartphones affected college students' study habits. He discovered students could only concentrate for three minutes at a stretch on average.

Rosen's study also found that multitasking students (those changing tasks frequently) who were interrupted only once during fifteen minutes of testing were likely to be poor students. He went on to state, "Students reported that even without the constant reminders provided by notification lights and sounds, they were internally preoccupied with whether anyone was trying to get in touch with them or commenting on their statuses."

So it seems the scales are tilted toward technology being a detriment to mainstream society in many ways, including education, social interactions, personal relationships, and in the workplace.

Yet, there are those supporting the contrary side. Business News Daily recently reported on The Harford's Tech@Work Survey. It polled more than 1,200 employed U.S. adults who said their productivity is improved by the internet, email, and mobile devices.

This really is no surprise. These services have dramatically improved the way we do business today.

Many workers could not perform their jobs adequately, or at all, without them. Why, imagine if the world abandoned computers or using the internet?

But it has been estimated that as much as 71 percent of office workers abuse the internet during working hours by visiting social networking sites, shopping online, reading personal emails, or playing games. One or more hours each day of lost productivity can be attributed to this.

The American Psychology Association (APA) states, "This attachment to devices and the constant use of technology is associated with higher stress levels for Americans. Generally, nearly one-fifth of Americans (18 percent) identify the use of technology as a very or somewhat significant source of stress."

Based on all these statistical studies, we must learn to better manage our use of technology and smart devices in order to perform more effectively and reduce harmful stress. We have to learn to resist the temptation to respond instantly to any number of technological stimuli when it is not related to our job performance or conducive to building personal relationships.

In many cases, this is just a learned habit that needs to be broken. We have become conditioned to these chimes, bells, and alerts. Once we discover ways of overcoming the temptations to respond to these alerts when not necessary or when it is not in the best interest of our family, friends, or ourselves, then life will invite us to experience more meaningful events and relationships.

While visiting friends one evening, I noticed a group of younger friends in their thirties playing cards. During the entire game, each of the four was engaged in texting. There was hardly a minute that one of them was not texting someone.

None of them were fully engaged with each other or with the game they were playing. There were countless opportunities to interact with each other in more meaningful ways, but they were all enveloped in their private worlds, unaware of their failure to be totally present and connected with each other.

Many times each day, while fully engaged in conversation with me, I experience employees allowing themselves to interrupt our conversation with their smartphones. They will pause in the middle of a statement to check their device or they will rudely reply to a text or email while I am speaking. And this behavior is not limited to me.

Over the last several years, I have observed many business men and women rudely employ the use of smart devices routinely while interacting with others. I'll admit I am not immune. I have personally succumbed to the temptation of responding to texts while conversing with others more times than I care to remember.

It is sad that most do not realize they are belittling their social interaction with each other while engaging in another conversation or information exchange using their devices. This disrespectful attention thief is all too common, not only in our business world, but in our personal relationships as well.

Smart devices are among the worst culprits of attention depletion. The instant reminders, sounds, and visuals tend to draw our attention away from those around us. We find ourselves relying on the devices for immediate knowledge and answers.

The very structure of our universe may well be data-based. We are natural data exchangers. But now more than ever, we process enormous amounts of information at any given moment. The current barrage of data from television, radio, smartphones, and computers is more than anyone has ever experienced in the history of our civilization. But this has consequences.

Our ability to rely on our intuition that expresses our inner guidance system and our higher sense of self is diminished when we depend on our voice-activated, artificial intelligence software program on our smart devices.

Instead of relying on our memory and our brain's knowledge bank, we often just ask our smartphone friend Siri or smart home device Alexa. It's quick,

easy, convenient, and available. If we cannot come up with the answers we need on our own, why not just ask our computerized intelligent personal assistant? It is because it reduces the personal elements of life. It conditions us to rely on mechanical devices rather than the natural gifts of intelligence and the innately human qualities of interconnectedness and emotional responses.

Relying excessively on technology can lead to a reduced capacity to derive solutions to questions or problems we encounter daily. It's similar to answering all the questions of your child or student instead of challenging them to formulate their own conclusions while we provide constructive assistance.

Dependence on external mechanisms for solutions reduces our brain power and the capacity to make decisions based on our own judgments and conclusions. It weakens our mental flexibility, contributes to lethargy, and proliferates the over-reliance on external forces.

When we depend on our natural internal forces and abilities, our confidence level increases to meet our expectations. We realize a sense of satisfaction and self-reliance which results in a more gratifying experience of life. Simply stated, it's more fulfilling.

To keep the human approach alive in my life, I ask those around me for answers to my questions. It keeps my mind searching while connecting with other souls at the same time. It stimulates the working memory, and is mentally and socially healthy.

Exercising our minds is paramount to our mental and emotional development. It engenders means for producing elevated awareness, expanded neural pathways, and increased capacity for growth and improvement.

Our relationship with technology should be mutually beneficial. When we access websites to view a near-by restaurant, we are supporting businesses that create jobs and provide valuable services. Scheduling medical appointments or travel online can avoid the stress of trying to reach a representative on the phone, plus it can be done at your leisure when it's convenient for you.

When we use technology as a tool to assist us instead of allowing it to control us, then we place ourselves in a position of power. Mindfully accessing technology when necessary or when most convenient can be productive and satisfying. The problems begin when we find ourselves compulsively interacting with smart devices at every beckoning moment.

How often do you look at your phone during the day? Is it on your desk or on the counter in front of you, continually inviting your attention? Do you reach for your device each time you hear an alert to check your emails, texts, or calls? Do you feel compelled to respond immediately?

This compulsive behavior is an over-dependence on technology. It can overwhelm our senses and dilute our job performance. It can interfere with the connectedness of our relationships in ways we might not even notice.

Over-dependence on anything produces unwanted stress and complications. When our minds are dealing with the over-stimulation from technology and social media, we become distracted from the tasks at hand. We also lose valuable time shared with those we care about. When your attention is misdirected, you disrupt your flow of creativity and train of thought regarding your work or play, and it moves you away from the things and people in your life that are most worthwhile.

What's the answer?

We must learn to control our attention and the use of technology, making the deliberate decision to access our devices when we want to, not when these devices beckon us.

Just recently, I decided to reduce the role of my smartphone in my life. I unsubscribed to unimportant websites bombarding me with emails. I changed my phone settings to eliminate notification sounds, banners, and alerts, only leaving my personal reminders and calendars intact.

What an enormous amount of free time I realized as a result! I found my stress levels immediately reduced, and I actually felt lighter and freer. I don't feel compelled to instantly check my social media and emails any time there is a post. I check them when I decide to. It has been a most liberating experience, even more than what I expected.

We also need to consciously recognize opportunities to connect and communicate with people. Personal relationships are far more important than interacting with impersonal devices. When you are in the presence of someone whose desire is to be present with you, you must give them your undivided attention. This is how valuable relationships are forged and maintained.

Solutions

Tom Cronin is a meditation teacher, life mentor, speaker, writer, and producer. Here are some of his suggestions for shifting your awareness away from technology and bringing your attention under control.

• When you arrive home at night, put your phone on silent mode and place it out of sight. Set a time(s) to check your phone only to see if there are urgent messages. If there are none, then put the phone back out of sight.

• If you are taking a restroom, tea, or coffee break at work, leave your phone at your desk. Concentrate on stretching your legs and/or interacting with your coworkers.

• When you get in your car, place your phone in your glove box and on silent mode. Be present to the road, other vehicles, safety, and your journey with mindfulness.

• When you are out walking, bring your attention to the world around you. Look at the sky, the trees, the sun, feel the breeze. What do you smell, see, hear, taste, touch? Be conscious of not being distracted and pulling out your phone to text someone. Focusing on your environment will make you aware of how often you automatically reach for your phone. It's an eye-opener.

• When you are on public transport, set aside moments that are purposely free of interaction with your phone, including music. Look at the view on your journey. Likely, you will notice things you've never seen before. Take time to review your day just passed or plan the day ahead. You might find your commute becomes your creative time where you germinate your business ideas.

• Set aside time each day for meditation. These sessions of mental quietness are a powerful way to take a break from data absorption, and they promote psychological and physical rest. Take this time in solitude and stillness daily and focus just on you.

This may seem like a great deal of change to make all at once for some people. Try choosing one or two days a week at first to make some of these adjustments and then add to it. As you experience positive results, you will want to continue to a more expansive level.

A note to parents: Please observe your children's use of smart devices and control the amount of exposure.

Do some research on how these devices can affect your children. Many studies show overuse can be extremely detrimental to their health and development.

Resources

Jon Kabat-Zinn, Ph.D.: www.mindfulnesscds.com and or Sounds True: www.soundstrue.com. Both sites offer mindfulness and meditation CDs and information. Also, check out Jon's books: *Full Catastrophe Living; Wherever You Go, There You Are; and Mindfulness for Beginners.*

Tom Cronin: www.tomcronin.com. Tom offers mindfulness and meditation techniques.

Visit my website www.AwakenMyPotential.com. You can also read my short, best-selling book, *The Mindfulness Approach*.

Laura Silva Quesada: www.laurasilvaquesada.com. Laura explains her Silva Method for Meditation.

Time Magazine: www.time.com. Search for the article "We Need to Talk about Kids and Smartphones."

National Public Radio: www.npr.org. Search for the article "The Risk of Teen Depression and Suicide Is Linked to Smartphone Use, Study Says."

Reminder: You can find all live resource links on the author's website at AwakenMyPotential.com.

Chapter Five

Brain Chatter

How to Get into the Zone

Most people have an incessant dialog running constantly within their minds at any given moment. Some are working out a discussion they plan to have with their boss about a work issue. Others may be mentally reliving an argument with a family member.

This continuous brain chatter is responsible for elevating stress levels by monopolizing our attention. There is so much going on in our heads it distracts us from being present with the activities at hand. This relentless background noise can take control of our work or play. Instead of being present with our current situation, we become distracted by our own inner dialog (or monolog).

With a constant, flowing stream of mental conversation, data, or information, we can become easily overwhelmed. We may not even be aware of it because we have conditioned ourselves to this endless chatter for many years.

The pressure is on!

What happens when your computer becomes bogged down with too many programs running, or you have not taken time to clear the memory cache, or you have not updated your software? It becomes slow or locks up on you.

Our brains react similarly when we attempt to process more data than we are capable of while performing tasks. Information overload becomes the norm as we challenge ourselves to handle increasing amounts of external data while at the same time managing the attention-draining demands of our brain chatter. There's a limit to what we can endure.

We need to control the input of data so it does not control us. Although our brains are incredibly complex and can process information on levels we may not be aware of, there is a limit to what most of us mere mortals can endure given the fast pace of society and the world we live in.

Managing our attention is a crucial ingredient in operating at optimum performance levels during our work and play. Just being aware of the brain's chatter as often as possible will bring about opportunities to focus our attention on what interests us most at the time.

When we are self-absorbed and preoccupied with our past, present, or future failures and successes, we miss opportunities to capture the moment and complete our tasks with the total focus of a clear mind and an unstressed body.

To stop food from cooking, it needs to be removed from the heat. Remove yourself, at least partially, from the plethora of data and internal dialog and your mind will slow down, even if only a little. This will bring you more fully into the present.

The present moment is where the wonder of life exists in all its splendor. Being completely present, in the moment, opens the doors to complete fulfillment and satisfaction.

Get in Flow.

You've heard many professional athletes speak about this. "I was in the zone," they say in the post-game interviews. But what is being in the zone, sometimes also expressed as being in flow?

Being in the zone or being in flow refers to the gap or space between thoughts. This gap is where many creative impulses and intuitions are initiated. It is the mental state of action when a person is fully immersed in a feeling of energized focus. Flow can be characterized by complete absorption in any activity.

Being in the zone is more about being totally present while performing tasks rather than thinking about them. When you are in the flow, you are not consciously thinking about your responsibility. Instead, you are just doing it—anything from washing the car to painting a masterpiece—while expecting positive results. You are allowing your subconscious mind to take command.

In an IGN Sports interview with Kobe Bryant (2012), he was asked, "What was going through your head when you were scoring eighty-one points (just in the one game)?

Bryant replied, "Everything was happening in slow motion for me, and you just really want to stay in that moment. You don't want to step outside of yourself and think about what is going on because then you are going to lose that rhythm."

Bryant understands the power of mindfulness as taught to him, as well as Michael Jordan and Shaquille O'Neal, by meditation teacher/coach George Mumford. Mumford learned his techniques from studying under one of the world's preeminent mindfulness and meditation teachers, Jon Kabat-Zinn (who introduced me to the same).

In an ABC News interview (2016), Mumford explained his meditation techniques.

> It's more a monitoring aspect with more—rather than "I got to make this shot"—no just shoot. You've trained your nervous system to do it, so now your conscious thinking needs to be quiet and let your body do what it does… nothing exists but this moment and what you're doing.

> Meditation is not trying to go anywhere or do anything, meditation and being present is just seeing what's there and letting it speak to you. The goal is to be present to what is. … Can you create space where you can observe it without being identified with it?

Kobe Bryant also offered an explanation of "being in the zone" on a social video in 2012. He said:

> Everything slows down and you have this supreme confidence. You have to really try to stay in the present and not let anything break

that rhythm. You get in the zone and just kind of stay there. You become oblivious to everything that's going on. You don't think about your surroundings or what's going on with the crowd or the team.

Let me share a story from a lesser known athlete. My oldest daughter, Jenna, played on the basketball team in middle school for a single season. One of her best friends was an incredible athlete and the team's star player. I think Jenna joined the sport primarily to be with her friend and enjoy the social aspects of the team. My daughter is very athletic in some areas, but basketball was not her thing. She rarely made a basket.

I left work one day to attend a game and cheer Jenna and her team on. Just before the halfway point, one of the players blocked another's pass, and the ball took a detour into Jenna's hands at mid-court. The look on her face was one of complete surprise and, for a couple of seconds, mildly panicked bewilderment. She looked around at the other players as if she was hoping one of her team members would tell her what to do with the ball.

Then, without thinking, she just heaved the ball halfway across the court toward the basket. To her utter surprise and delight, the ball cleared the rim and plunged through the net for the three points, becoming the most incredible shot of the game. The crowd came to their feet and exploded with applause.

At that precise moment, Jenna was in the zone. Once she realized consciously thinking about what to do with the basketball was not working for her, she just let go and took the shot. This is what professional athletes do regularly, and it is what any of us can do too.

Superstar athletes just allow the moment to unfold. They let their minds and bodies work in complete synchronicity for their desired outcomes without giving thought to what they are doing and without being concerned with the final results.

The players tune out the cheering crowds, the announcers, and the music along with the chatter in their own minds so they can just be in the moment. It allows them to perform and compete to the very best of their abilities.

We all can perform this way in our personal and business lives, but it requires eliminating distractions just as elite athletes do. You know what I'm referring to—those annoying chimes from your smartphone, background conversations of those around us, the drone of the television, or any other distractions that impede our efforts. The more committed we are in the moment to making the very most of our time and talent, the higher the results we will realize.

Sometimes, while I am writing, I get so immersed in my work that I have no conception of time. I can work for three or more hours straight and think that only an hour has elapsed. *This is being in the zone.* I am engaged fully and completely. My mind doesn't wander and my attention is not easily diverted.

It's easy for some people to stay focused and get into the zone. For me, I often have to discipline myself with tremendous effort to stay focused on projects. I rely on the tools and processes that I teach to stay focused and remain in the flow.

When we are sharing time with family or friends, we should also strive to be in flow. We should pay meticulous attention to those around us and our conversations and interactions with them, just remaining in the present moment and allow our emotions and inner guidance to gently lead us into positive, sincere relations.

When our minds are divided into multiple layers of thoughts, issues, or problems, it is almost impossible to be in the flow. Our minds can only handle so many thoughts or objects of attention at a time.

A case in point: try focusing on a conversation you are having with someone while listening to someone else's discussion, all while writing a note as you simultaneously recite the lyrics of your favorite song.

If you can accomplish these four focal points of attention concurrently with proficiency, you are one rare and fantastic person. Most of us would only be readily attentive to one or two of the four without becoming distracted or frustrated. The more focal points of attention we attempt to hold at the same time, the less proficient we will be with any of them.

This is why distractions can deplete our energy and cause mental exhaustion. Bringing our attention repeatedly back to the present moment with constant practice and discipline will incur a sense of self-reliance and contentment. And isn't that what we all want?

Solutions

- Be aware of how many activities you are trying to do at once. Multi-tasking actually is an enemy of effective progress. Turn your attention to completing one item on your to-do list at a time, rather than flitting back and forth between them making partial efforts.

- Quiet your brain chatter with meditation, music, breathing, or whatever means that work for you so your intuition can come to fruition.

- Be in the present moment. Learn to feel your way through life. Feelings are more powerful than thoughts.

- Get out of your head and get into your gut more often. Balance your rational brain with your feeling mind. When you catch yourself over-analyzing, transition into observing your feelings.

- Act upon your intuitive impulses to navigate your way through situations. Feel, listen, and then act. Don't worry about making the wrong decision. Just be open and aware, observing the information that becomes available to you.

Resources

Harvard Business Review: www.hbr.org. Search for the article "How to Get into Your Zone."

Inc.: www.inc.com. Search for the article "3 Tricks to Help You Get in the Zone."

Jon Kabat-Zinn, Ph.D.: www.mindfulnesscds.com and Sounds True: soundstrue.com. Jon Each site offers mindfulness and meditation CDs and information. Also, check out Jon's books: *Full Catastrophe Living; Wherever You Go, There You Are;* and *Mindfulness for Beginners.*

Tom Cronin: www.tomcronin.com. Explore the mindfulness and meditation techniques he offers.

AwakenMyPotential.com: www.awakenmypotential.com. Read my short best-selling book, *The Mindfulness Approach.*

Reminder: You can find all live resource links on the author's website at AwakenMyPotential.com.

Chapter Six

Perception Becomes Reality

How Your Beliefs Control Your Life

When does perception become a reality? Isn't that a question many have pondered? Here is my answer: as soon as you have decided what you are perceiving is real and is your truth, then it becomes your reality— what appears as most real to you.

We frequently make instant decisions about what we perceive, and those decisions are generally based on our belief systems. Our beliefs influence our viewpoints on virtually everything. For instance, you may believe that men who wear sleeveless, tank top T-shirts are "wife beaters" due to past notorious criminals' use of them as portrayed in news media and movies. This belief can cause you to fear men in tank-top shirts.

Most of our beliefs were initially formed when we were under the age of ten. Here's an example to illustrate how perception can become one's reality. Let's consider a boy attending elementary school who is smaller in size than average. He is bullied on the playground several days in a row by boys much bigger than him, and he forms a belief that playgrounds are dangerous.

When his friends later ask to meet him at a playground near his home, away from school, he becomes wary and fearful as he approaches the grounds. His fear rises from his new belief that playgrounds are dangerous. Even though he is with his friends at the moment, the fear is still genuine to him.

The next day, the boy had forgotten there was going to be a history test, and therefore failed the test. The other students in the class laughed and made fun of him. He was so embarrassed and humiliated he was ashamed to show up at school the following day.

This series of events had a powerful impact on the boy's perception of his school. Now he viewed the playgrounds as dangerous and the classroom as a place of shame. He had no idea he had created two beliefs that would alter the course of his life.

Later in high school, the boy abstained from sports and became shy and reserved in the classroom. He was private about his grades and became extremely defensive about his test scores with his parents, even when his ratings were just below perfect. His long-held beliefs became his present reality.

Each of us has an opportunity, at any time, to re-assess our beliefs and perceptions. If we can discover the event or events that prompted us to create nega-tive beliefs, then we can find ways of eliminating them and creating new beliefs.

The most important thing to understand is that events do not cause beliefs. Events are just things that occur. Things that happen do not create beliefs. It is our *per-ception* of the events that create beliefs. We just need to learn to separate the events from the way we view them.

In many cases, several beliefs can be generated from one event. In the example above, the young boy created the belief that playgrounds are dangerous. He may also have developed beliefs that boys bigger than him are bullies, that bigger boys are tough and inconsiderate, that he is a coward and weak or unworthy, and that girls won't like him due to his weaknesses.

We each have a multitude of beliefs that interfere with our perceptions of people and events. Once we come to the realization that our beliefs are guiding us through life, we can learn how to change them to benefit us. When we get to the point where we can see an event without judging it based on our past experiences, then we will be able to view it in a different light.

What if you saw a news program that showed a person losing their job due to an illness? Most people would feel sad and sorry for this person. But what if this person was in a place in their life where they needed to learn a lesson of this sort? Would that change your reaction?

What if during the next week they received the job of their dreams? Losing their job may have been the very thing they needed to move to the next level in life. What if their health issue resolved due to having new and better insurance coverage, and they are now happier and more content with their new job? Now how would you perceive the loss of the initial job?

Allowing events to negatively influence the way we feel is not beneficial to our wellbeing. On a daily basis, we can become overwhelmed with self-deprecating, erroneous emotional responses to events we may be judging and labeling inappropriately.

Beliefs are merely constructs within your mind. If they are not real in the sense that you can see, smell, hear, or touch them, then they are only labels you created within your own mind. This means that you can change your original opinion of the situation.

Even though most people think they can either see or feel these limiting beliefs, they are really just seeing the memory of the event in their mind or feeling the emotions associated with it.

The meaning we ascribe to events depends on many things, such as our attitude at the time, our outlook on life, our current situation, our past beliefs, and our relationship to the event or individuals involved. It is only the meaning we assign to events that determines how we respond to them.

It is possible, and important, to see events just as they are—as events, nothing more. We simply need to view different aspects of the events in a non-judgmental, open-minded way.

I am reminded of my dog Klara, a small, blonde Vizsla. Sunday is bath day for Klara. During the summer, she can easily be coaxed into our outdoor shower where we use comfortable, warm water from a handheld shower head to bathe her.

However, during the winter, when it is cold outside, it's a different story. Inside our warm home, I mention to her that it is bath time and her shoulders begin to shake. Within one minute, her entire body is shivering.

Now, I don't think we can reasonably consider that a dog can hold a belief the way a human can, but it is a similar situation. She knows what a bath is, and she experiences trepidations upon the thought of being wet out in the cold. Fundamentally, she believes it will be a cold, wet event.

Have you ever visualized tasting a lemon? We can experience the same sensations with visualization. If you take a moment and really feel what it is like in your mind to bite the inside of a lemon, you may salivate profusely and your face may even pucker as if you were actually eating a real lemon. The thought became the physical experience—instantly!

The way we respond to our beliefs of past events is similar in that we can experience a multitude of emotions like fear, horror, sadness, guilt, and anger, or conversely, elation, happiness, hope, and love. Bringing a past emotionally charged event to mind can trigger deep feelings along with matching changes in physiology. The beliefs that we have created regarding past events can alter our current mental, emotional, and physical states of being.

I'll provide a quote from my first book, *The Experiential Approach*: "When a notion is converted into a solid belief, the creative power of the Universe is unleashed, and the manifestation of a miracle is at hand."

Quite possibly, the most significant power we possess is that of belief. A thought is just something that enters our minds, but a belief is a thought we have transformed into something that carries considerable weight. Yet, we can change our beliefs at any time. It is the power of being able to make that change that will free you from any harmful events of the past.

There are many ways to change or eliminate undesirable beliefs, and it is called belief management. The Lefkoe Method program, ReCreate Your Life, is one that I am particularly fond of.

The Lefkoe Method (TLM) provides a simple method of transforming the old negative beliefs determining our thoughts, feelings, and behaviors into harmless bits of data. TLM posits a belief is a statement about reality that feels true on some level. Our thoughts become beliefs that then become accurate statements about our perceived reality.

At an early age, our beliefs were created from the way our parents *reacted* to our behavior. For instance, our parents may have become annoyed when we did not do what they wanted when and in the way they wanted. It is our interpretation of how our parents reacted when we did not behave according to their wishes that has led to a currently held belief.

But realize, we may have generated only one of many interpretations of their irritations. Our interpretation may not have been the truth. We may have only recognized one of many perceptions of reality.

At the time of an event, we might have thought we could see the belief or at least feel it. Actually, it was only a construct within our mind.

We looked at events that could have had many different meanings and we chose one. We then solidified that in our mind. Each time we attributed our meaning (how our parents reacted) to an event, it was as if we could actually see the belief.

We did not actually see the meaning in the event, we ascribed our meaning to it. The event had no meaning before we gave it one. It was as if we saw the event the same as seeing the meaning.

Anything we can see can be described by its shape, color, and location. What did our belief look like when we were a child? Could we see the shape, color, or location? Of course not.

The event we experienced had no meaning until we gave it one. Meaning is only in our mind, so there could be no meaning to your parents' behavior or the event itself. It is only our interpretation of our parents' behavior that helped us create the belief. It's not that the event did not matter to us, it just had no meaning in and of itself.

Our parents' behavior or displeasure with us may have led to our feeling bad, and we related that to the event. However, our parents could not have made us feel bad because that is only something that we could have done.

We create our own feelings. Events are meaningless and cannot make us feel anything. They are just events, things that happen. Events themselves cannot produce any feelings.

We form beliefs to give meaning to events that have no real meaning. Once we fully grasp this concept, our lives can experience meaningful change. Can you identify a belief that may be limiting you?

Solutions

- Understand the importance of beliefs and how they impact your life and direct your path. Read chapter eleven to learn how to eliminate negative beliefs and to create new empowering beliefs.

- Discover beliefs that may be holding you back and eliminate them.

- Become aware of your pre-conceived notions about how things appear to you.

- Learn to view situations and events with an open mind and heart.

- Create new beliefs that empower you to move toward your goals.

Deepak Chopra suggests opening your awareness to your strongest beliefs, your core beliefs. In this way, you can find out who you are and what drives you to behave in the ways you do. He states new energies emerge when you pursue core beliefs that are life-supporting, fulfilling, and spiritually transforming.

Chopra maintains there are four core beliefs in the areas of love, self-worth, security, and fulfillment. He suggests you activate and internalize the following:

1. I am loving and lovable.
2. I am worthy.
3. I am safe and trusting.
4. I am fulfilled and whole.

The change you desire must come at the level of self-awareness where your true self resides. Reliving your past only keeps you stuck in the past. Your core beliefs are activated in the present and can only be changed in the present, right now. Here is what Dr. Chopra recommends:

- Look upon what's happening now as a reflection of your core beliefs.

- If the reflection is negative, pause and ask yourself why it fits the storyline that your beliefs create. If you experience any kind of abusive treatment, for example, this reflects a victimhood story supported by a core belief that keeps you in the story. If you experience unexpected kindness, on the other hand, this demonstrates a storyline that includes compassion and a core belief in how much you deserve love.

- Whenever you get any hint of the story you are living, tell yourself that you don't need stories. You only need to live in the present moment.

- In the present moment, your true self is trying to bring you closer to an improved level of love, self-worth, trust, and wholeness. Keep that in mind as your daily vision and remind yourself that you are always moving in this direction.

Resources

Activebeat: www.activebeat.com. Search for the article "Jumping to Conclusions: 6 Ways Perception Affects Our Lives."

Psychology Today: www.psychologytoday.com. Search for the article "Perception Is Not Reality."

Deepak Chopra: www.deepakchopra.com. The Chopra Center. Search for the page: Managing Beliefs.

The Lefkoe Institute: www.lefkoe.com. Managing belief systems audio programs.

Tony Robbins: www.tonyrobbins.com. Search for the page: Beliefs.

Reminder: You can find all live resource links on the author's website at AwakenMyPotential.com.

Chapter Seven

Neutralize Your Past Negative Events

How Beliefs Conform to Your Labels

One morning at work, you pass an unfamiliar employee in the hallway who has just transferred into your department. You say "good morning and welcome" to him, and he glances up and does not respond. Immediately, you label him as a "snob" and tell your fellow employees about the new snob who ignored your welcoming remarks. "What a jerk!" you declare.

Later that afternoon, you pass him once again in the hallway and ask him why he did not acknowledge you earlier. He responds apologetically, explaining his job position abruptly changed that morning without his knowledge and he was so distracted and disappointed he did not even realize you spoke to him. He apologized and said he felt terrible about not responding and hoped you would understand and forgive him.

You now feel horrible about the things you said about him to the other employees and hope he does not find out about them. You realize the labels "snob" and "jerk" you gave him were inappropriate and unkind.

So many times, we are quick to judge others and events, and we label them as we perceive them at the time. Labeling can not only be damaging to others, but it can also be very destructive to ourselves as well.

Once you label something, you have created a permanent record of it within your mind, and another person's brain, too, if they are aware of it. When we can move away from labeling people, situations, and events, then we will not encumber ourselves and others with these descriptions, which instantly become beliefs.

When you placed those labels of "snob" and "jerk" on the new employee, you immediately created a belief that he is such. Of course, you changed that belief later when you discovered the facts behind the event.

A more dramatic example of how labeling can lead to lasting beliefs might involve a situation where you were roughly handled by a parent as a child. Suppose, at age six, while crossing the parking lot at a local shopping mall, you wander a few feet from your parents, then your father firmly grabs you by the arm and drags you toward him while yelling at you.

He then spanks you very hard while sternly scolding you, telling you that you are stupid and careless. You are scared, crying, and notice others are watching with dismay. You are horrified and embarrassed and feel at that moment your father does not love you.

You label him as "mean" and decide you hate him for treating you this way. From this point forward, you fear him and your relationship changes to a degree. Your new beliefs are that your father does not love you and that he is mean.

Your behavior from this moment on is determined by your new beliefs as a result of your labeling. Anytime you are away from home with your father, you are afraid of what he might do to you if you make a mis-

86

take or forget to pay close attention to your actions. You are now driven by fear.

So, what are the facts? You unknowingly strayed from your father's side. You were scolded severely. You were spanked angrily. You were told you were stupid and careless.

In your mind, you were only a few feet from your father, you were safe, you were not misbehaving, and you were where you thought you were supposed to be. You felt you did nothing wrong and your father was to blame. He is mean, he does not love you, and you hate him for it. You feel abandoned.

If you had been able to look at this incident without emotion as simply an event, and did not label it with your judgments, you might have experienced a different outcome. Even now, if you look back on this scene as just an event—something that happened— without judgment, you may be able to change the way you remember it and, more importantly, the way you feel about it.

Let's explore the possibility of envisioning alternative viewpoints of past negatively charged events.

What if your mother and father were having an argument just before the incident in the shopping mall parking lot? What if your father was angry at the time about something that did not involve you? What if your father had seen a child hit by a car prior to that day and the child had died on the scene? What if your father loved you so much and was so scared of losing you that he could not contain his emotions and reacted to an extreme?

Even if your father was wrong for what he did, it did not mean he did not love you. Perhaps he acted based on what he felt was best for you to keep you safe. What if he was treated that way by his father and that was the only way he knew to respond to the situation?

When you are able to step back and view the past event differently, you are in a position to change how you feel about it now, and from this point forward.

Each time you remember this past situation, using the "what ifs" from above, you can reframe it. You can run the movie in your mind from the perspective of your father, mother, or those witnessing it. View various possibilities and outcomes. Rewind it the way you want to see it.

If you looked at it from the perspective of those witnesses in the parking lot, some of those people might have been concerned for your safety too. They may have thought your parents were not paying close attention to your whereabouts and thought your father's actions were justified once he realized you were straying too far.

You can replay any event many ways. The more you create videos in your mind of other viewpoints and how you would prefer to remember it, the less power the negatively charged event has over you. Each time you return to the event, the other movies you constructed in your mind will dilute the original event, and the emotional charge will be reduced until rendered harmless.

You have the power to virtually change your past. It is only a memory, and memories can fool us at times. We remember them based on the emotional charge of the situation. The more intense the emotion at the time, the more fixed the event becomes in our minds. These strong feelings actually embed themselves in our cellular being and can cause long-term health issues if not resolved.

You want to be able to reframe situations to your advantage. This involves looking at issues in a new light with a different perspective. I am not saying to deny the existence or difficulty of a situation. Rather, I want to encourage you to view it in a way that invites you to find positive meaning and introspection. I want you to get to the point where you can ask, "What can I learn from this?"

Reframing is another technique you can use to reduce the emotional charge of a past negative event. You can view a current or past adverse event in your mind as if it had a black picture frame around it. Then, replace the picture frame with another one of your choosing. It may be more decorative, fun, colorful, or bright. Once you change the frame, realize that you can change the way you see the event within your mind as well.

If we change our thoughts, we change our lives!

Solutions

• Practice utilizing the reframing technique mentioned above.

• Understand the importance of beliefs and how they impact your life and direct your path. Discover beliefs that may be holding you back and eliminate them.

• Create new beliefs that empower you to move toward your goals.

• Revisit The Lefkoe Method (TLM) discussed in chapter six. I am particularly fond of TLM as it provides a simple method of transforming old negative beliefs into harmless bits of data.

Resources

Deepak Chopra: www.deepakchopra.com. The Chopra Center. Search for the page: Managing Beliefs.

Psychology Today: www.psychologytoday.com. Search for the article "Reframing."

AwakenMyPotential.com: www.awakenmypotential.-com. Also, read my short book, *The Experiential Approach*.

Reminder: You can find all live resource links on the author's website at AwakenMyPotential.com.

Chapter Eight

Perspective

How to Shift Yourself into Positivity

I'm sure you've heard the phrase "let's put things into perspective." What does that actually mean, though? Is it about putting things into a specific frame of reference or frame of mind? Is it about adopting another viewpoint or alternative interpretation? Or does it just refer to a way of looking at something?

Perspective can be all of this and more. When you put things into perspective, you have a choice of using your own perspective or applying someone else's. Some people can be easily influenced by other's views and make decisions based on them.

Sheep follow other sheep blindly over the cliff every day without giving thought to their own perspective of the path they are on. I believe it was George S.

Patton who said, "We herd sheep, we drive cattle, we lead people. Lead me, follow me, or get out of my way."

All too often, we embrace the ideals of others without giving regard to our own internal guidance. We either jump to unfounded conclusions or we are inequitably influenced by the status of another.

At times we agree with others' beliefs before we take the time to examine the facts and seek advice from our own hearts and minds. It is sometimes easier to conform and adopt the position of someone else to feel accepted and popular.

Our perspective also can be dependent upon our attitude. The way we view situations and events is influenced dynamically by our attitude because our approach in that instance is primarily emotion-based. This is opposed to when we view things rationally, which is more cognitive based.

If you have a positive attitude about your employer and your working conditions, you will likely not react strongly about negative events or changes that occur in your workplace. For instance, your boss belittles you in front of a peer and you brush it off as your boss's inability to lead effectively. It's your boss's problem, not yours.

Conversely, if you maintain a negative attitude, then you may react with anger, frustration, or become distressed more easily. Regarding the same situation above, you take it personally and become angry. In this negative state of mind, you now have trouble focusing on your current tasks.

Our attitudes can positively or adversely alter the course of our lives. Much has been said about maintaining a positive attitude. It may be far more difficult for some people than others to keep an upbeat outlook. It also may be more difficult to do so in certain situations.

Wouldn't it be ideal to experience every situation that arises in a positive manner?

The opening paragraph of a martial arts creed that I taught for many years states, "I intend to develop myself in a positive manner and avoid anything that will reduce my mental and spiritual growth or physical health."

It would be great to avoid the negatives in life but they are all around us, attempting to affect the outcomes of our lives. The keyword in this section of the creed is *intend.* When our intentions are powerful and sincere, we have a more exceptional ability to withstand the onslaught of negative situations and negative people.

While we may not be able to avoid detrimental situations, we can choose to respond in positive ways. A positive solution is always better than a negative answer. When we embrace a positive attitude as often as we can, then we open ourselves to the possibilities of gratifying outcomes.

How might keeping a positive attitude affect your experience visiting a local state park with a friend during a holiday weekend?

You and your friend have worked long hours under stressful conditions for the last few days, and you are both ready to unwind and relax. When you arrive at the park, however, you come face to face with a more than half-mile long line of cars at the gate, and you realize it may take most of an hour just to get inside.

Immediately, your heart rate and blood pressure increase, and you feel a surge of irritation and anxiety flowing through your veins. Your anticipation of a fun, relaxing day at the park just vanished into an abyss of negativity.

"I knew we shouldn't have come here on a holiday weekend. This was a stupid idea. We'll waste half our morning just trying to get inside," you utter angrily. Your friend reassures you it won't take that long and that maybe you both could use the time to check out the park's activities and trails. Your friend takes advantage of technology and explores the park's website on her smartphone.

During the thirty-five minute wait, however, you're pleased to discover many things about the park neither of you knew before your visit. There are far more activities, like canoeing, fishing, swimming, and hiking trails, than you were aware of.

While waiting in line, you explore the different trail routes online and decide which one you are going to hike. Now you know which direction to go once you are in the park so you can proceed directly to your chosen trail.

This story is a typical example of situations my wife and I often experience. Of course, I'm the anxious, impatient one and my wife is the one figuring out how to make the most of our idle time waiting in a proficient, positive manner. How easy it can be, at times, to forget to be positive and look for the possibilities of goodness in situations.

A slight shift in perception can mean the difference between experiencing a stressful, frustrating situation or feeling satisfied and relaxed with your current circumstances.

Remaining open to all choices and possibilities can provide pathways for positive, meaningful experiences. If we monitor our mental state and feelings, and then search our hearts for alternative methods of handling the situation at hand, we can discover a multitude of opportunities for positive outcomes.

It's about being mindful. We need to be aware of our reactions to stressful events. It's important to realize our perspective on the activity is what is causing us distress and not the event itself.

Why is it that your friend, who was with you in line at the state park, did not feel stressed or concerned about the long wait? Your friend's perspective was positive. She viewed this as an opportunity to explore the activities of the park and plan your visit so you could be efficient and have more time to hike the trail and have fun.

Remaining in a positive state of mind as much as possible is essential, however, we should embody all aspects of life, including both positive and negative experiences. The two are both a part of our daily walk through life. Don't be so positive that you distance yourself from others. You do not want to isolate yourself from those around you, making them feel that you may be unapproachable.

In other words, don't try to push negative feelings away from you. What you resist tends to persist. Accept your feelings as they are without judging them. Then, gently shift your awareness toward positive possibilities by asking yourself "How can I turn this situation into something I can learn from or that can benefit me?"

Sometimes we can alienate others by being overtly positive—especially if we are preaching it to others. It is far better to demonstrate a positive attitude with your behavior than it is to tell others to be positive.

Shifting perspectives can be challenging when you are in the grasp of anger or frustration. This is when it is the toughest for me. It really requires my taking a deep breath or two and asking if I truly want to feel angry or frustrated. I have to step back, quiet my mind for a moment, and allow other choices to present themselves.

Another great question to ask yourself when working to change your perspective is, "What can I do to make the most of this situation?" That opens the opportunity for your mind to search for ways to improve your circumstances. Of course, then you must act on one of those positive choices.

Solutions

Here are five simple suggestions for bringing yourself back into a positive state of mind:

- *Be grateful.* Feeling gratitude is a fast way to move into being positive and shift your focus away from negativity, judgment, and disappointment. Bring to mind things you are grateful for, like your family and friends, your health, the home you live in, the food you eat, your pet(s), your automobile, the clothes you wear, or your job. Anything you sincerely appreciate will cause gratitude to positively color your view.

- Smile. If you can force a smile on your face, even when you don't feel like it, you can trick your mind and body into feeling happy, especially if you can maintain that smile for a few moments. See how others react to your smile too. When another person smiles back at you, you will feel happier. Smile yourself into feeling good.

- *Be Kind.* Be kind to those around you. When you find yourself in the grasp of negativity, do something kind for someone else. Offer a compliment or a kind gesture. Go out of your way to help a coworker with a project or make a phone call to a friend or family member who needs some encouragement.

- *Hang out with positive people.* Positivity can be infectious. Find someone who generally has a positive attitude and hook up with them. Just being in the presence of a positive person can affect your state of mind.

- *Posture yourself for positivity.* The act of changing your posture can have a profound effect on your attitude. Your mind and body work in synchronicity, and one can easily affect the other. Stand up straight with your shoulders back and walk as if you were on the most important mission of your life, like others are depending on you to be the most positive, influential person they know.

• *Change your perspective.* Try to view the situation from the other person's perspective without judging them.

Resources

ActiveBeat: www.activebeat.com. Search for the article "6 Ways Perception Affects Our Lives."

CNN: www.cnn.com. Search for the article "The Power of Perceptions: Imagining the Reality You Want."

Inc Magazine: www.inc.com. Search for the article "Change Your Perspective, Change Your Life."

The Oprah Magazine: www.oprahmag.com. Search for the article "12 Ways to Instantly Become a More Positive Person."

Reminder: You can find all live resource links on the author's website at AwakenMyPotential.com.

Chapter Nine

A Life Changing Secret

How To Defeat Excessive Stress For Good

One of the most crucial elements of life is having a quick recovery. The very best thing you can do for yourself is to recover quickly from negative thoughts and events. This can be the most significant step of massive change you can make in your life.

Any experience that sets you back, angers or frustrates you, devastates you mentally or emotionally, causes you sorrow or pain, or makes you feel inadequate or unworthy is a potential stressor.

Undoubtably, you have experienced many of the following, perhaps on a daily basis: driving in traffic, an argument, offensive remarks, failing at something, repeating a bad habit, trying to master something complicated, feeling unable to control your emotions, being embarrassed, or feeling guilty or ashamed.

These negative experiences and emotions are at the forefront of many health concerns. Most chronic issues are related to stress stemming from old emotional wounds and current unfavorable home or work conditions.

Stress has an impact on almost every system in your body. It negatively affects the musculoskeletal, respiratory, cardiovascular, endocrine, gastrointestinal, nervous, and reproductive systems in various ways. Stress triggers the release of adrenaline, cortisol, and other hormones which increase heart rate and respiration, inducing a "fight or flight" reaction.

The "fight or flight" reaction is perfectly normal if danger presents itself or you are involved in competitive sports. Short bursts of these chemicals can help you survive or improve your immediate performance. However, an overabundance of stress can lead to an overload of adrenaline, cortisol, and hormones which can produce more harm than good in the long run.

Living in a constant state of "fight or flight" can cause extensive damage and put you at considerable risk of heart disease, stroke, obesity, or diabetes. Psychology Today cites a Harvard Business Review study (2012) that estimated between 60 and 90 percent of all doctor's visits are stress related.

The magazine also mentioned a Yale study that found stress caused by adverse life events reduced grey matter in the prefrontal cortex, the region of the brain responsible for self-control and emotion regulation. This reduction in brain volume has been linked to mood disorders, depression, anxiety, and an increase in risk-taking behavior and substance abuse.

The longer we linger in states of negativity and stress, the greater the propensity for long-term health issues. No one can afford to allow stress to command their life. Stress can bring the most powerful, confident individual to his knees if it is unacknowledged and ignored. Therefore, it's important to put ourselves in a position of power to control our mental, emotional, and physical wellbeing.

If we spend more than just a few minutes marinating in our miseries, we risk damage to our wellbeing. This damage may be physical, emotional, or mental. It is not worth experiencing the likelihood of partial or permanent harm to our systems.

What the mind harbors, the body manifests.

Here is what the American Psychology Association(APA) reports about the physical affects stress has on the body in a 2006 article titled "Americans Engage in Unhealthy Behaviors to Manage Stress."

People experiencing stress are more likely to report hypertension, anxiety or depression, and obesity. In particular, women report feeling the effects of stress on their physical health more than men. The survey results seem to tie in with what research shows, that 43 percent of all adults suffer adverse health effects from stress.

The article goes on to state that people experiencing stress are more likely to report specific ailments and symptoms.

- 59 percent report feeling nervous or sad
- 51 percent report symptoms of fatigue
- 56 percent report inability to sleep or sleeping too much
- 55 percent report lack of interest, motivation, or energy
- 46 percent report headaches
- 48 percent report muscular tension
- 32 percent report frequent upset stomach or indigestion
- 23 percent report change in sex drive

The APA also called out the unhealthy ways people deal with the above symptoms. "Americans engage in unhealthy behaviors such as comfort eating, poor diet choices, smoking and inactivity to help deal with stress." To state it simply, it is far more comfortable when you are stressed out to rely on unhealthy habits than it is when you are feeling relaxed and happy. We are attracted to the quick fixes of instant comfort.

I'm sure you can see this behavior in others, if not yourself. So many relieve the pressure of stress by drinking alcohol, smoking cigarettes, and eating unhealthy foods, with sweets leading the consumption. These means of coping with stress only serve to exacerbate symptoms. Most people realize a healthy diet and exercise are critical factors in reducing excess stress but they do not adjust their lifestyles in this manner.

It takes careful planning and discipline to avoid over-indulgence in unhealthy behaviors. Decisions about altering your diet and exercise should be made when you are in a relaxed, comfortable state of mind when rational thinking is optimal. This way, when a stressful situation arises, you are in a position to defer to previously set goals or intentions.

An important thing to keep in mind is no one can cause us to be stressed. As discussed earlier, we create our stress by how we view situations. If we do not like the situation we are in, then we must go about finding ways of changing the situation or simply changing the way we look at it.

Let's be clear about something. It is ok to experience negative events and emotions. You cannot go through life without encountering them. It's not smart to ignore them or refuse to feel them. We should experience them fully and allow the emotions to run their course. Refusing to face such issues causes ongoing health concerns since burying the anguish deep within our cellular being causes it to resurface again and again.

Remember, what we resist persists!

We only need to be aware of the times we have succumbed to stressful events and become stuck in negative emotions. Once we recognize we have become fixated on a situation, it is time to let it go. Of course, concerning the death of a loved one, there is a period of grieving that may take longer for some than others. The entire process of grieving must be experienced to allow for resolution.

So, what specific steps can we take to snap out of a negative, stressful event?

We can develop an attitude of the silent witness. When we find ourselves in the grasp of negative emotion, we can step back and take a look from a different perspective. View the situation as an observer just witnessing what is going on at the time. Just the act of changing perspective allows for the freedom of choice.

This way you will realize that the real you is in charge and not your emotions. You are the one behind the scenes controlling the buttons being pushed.

Dr. Deepak Chopra says it quite nicely.

> Therefore, the key to freedom is to become the silent witness, which is the ever-present awareness that witnesses everything. The silent witness is awareness itself. Awareness, aware of itself, is presence, profound wisdom, and peace. When you are free, you identify with your inner-self instead of your self-image. And within this freedom lies the ability to spontaneously put your attention on those

choices that bring joy to you, and also joy to others.

EMDR

Francine Shapiro, Ph.D. developed Eye Movement Desensitization and Reprocessing, shortened to EMDR, in 1989 as a psychotherapy treatment initially designed to alleviate distress associated with memories of traumatic experiences.

EMDR has been proven effective in providing relief by reformulating negative beliefs with subsequent physiological arousal reduction. The therapy utilizes repetitive lateral eye movements as an external stimulus while the patient attends to personal, emotionally disturbing material in brief sequential doses.

EMDR is as an empirically validated treatment of trauma and other adverse life experiences, so much so that the Department of Veterans Affairs' Practice Guidelines have placed it in the highest treatment category, recommended for all trauma populations at all times.

In addition, the International Society for Traumatic Stress Studies has designated EMDR as an effective treatment for PTSD (Foa, Keane, Friedman, and Cohen, 2009). EMDR was particularly beneficial to me in processing the trauma of a horrendous automobile accident that happened to me. The treatment allowed me to become desensitized to the feelings of physical and mental dysfunction that were plaguing me regarding the injuries I sustained.

Through multiple sessions, I was able to become desensitized to the extreme sensitivity of light and sound, and the depression I was experiencing. The practitioner would invite me to think about the accident and watch a bar containing a series of lights that moved horizontally from left to right, back and forth, for thirty seconds or so.

I relived the experience in my mind with all the emotions attached to it along with physical sensations. With each sensation that arose, I continued with another round of the light bar. At the end of each thirty minute session, I was quite relieved and felt more in control. I was able to function at an elevated level.

The therapy assisted me with reprocessing the stressors of physical and psychological dysfunction contained within my mind and body. When I completed treatment, I felt lighter, freer, and more capable of continuing life normally with fewer distractions of discomfort and mental distress. It was an amazing breakthrough of which I am incredibly grateful.

Tapping

Tapping is a combination of ancient Chinese acupressure and modern psychology working together to physically alter your brain, energy system, and your body simultaneously. It is also referred to as Emotional Freedom Technique or EFT. Instead of using applied pressure as in acupressure, the body's energy points are tapped several times by the individual while he concentrates on accepting and resolving the negative emotion, bad memory, or unresolved problem.

The acupoint tapping directly sends signals to the stress centers of the mid-brain temporal lobes (where the amygdala is located) bypassing the frontal lobes which are the thinking parts of the brain. So, in traditional talk therapy, the frontal lobes are engaged and the thinking process is stimulated. With EFT, the emotional centers of the brain are directly stimulated. EFT addresses stress on physical and emotional levels allowing individuals relief from some symptoms.

Tapping has worked well for me in some areas of my life. I have used it to reduce frustration and anxiety during extremely hectic times at work. A huge advantage of tapping is that it can be learned easily with little or no expense. There are many websites, including YouTube videos, that give free lessons and demonstrations.

Solutions

Try some or all of the following steps to recover quickly from the stressful effects of adverse events or situations.

- *Acknowledge your situation and feel it.* Never resist your feelings. Always realize, mentally or verbally, your negative situation, and feel your emotions in the moment. Be angry, frustrated, hurt, or whatever comes up and acknowledge the way you feel. You may even say to yourself, "It's ok to feel this way, I'm angry." You can set a time limit on your feelings, say five or ten minutes, and, once your time has expired, move yourself into more positive thoughts of how you want to feel.

- *Don't judge yourself or your feelings.* Remember, this is only an event, not you. You are the one viewing the event or situation. If you label your feelings as bad and something you don't want to feel, then you open the door to resistance. What you resist persists and gets buried deep within you.

117

- *Share your feelings.* Sometimes it helps to share your situation with another person without it just becoming a complaint session. Speak with a trusted friend or coworker and express your feelings. They may offer helpful advice. Also, it may help to speak your situation out loud to yourself. Many times a resolution to a negative event will come to light when you have a conversation with yourself about it.

- *Look to the future.* Ask yourself what you can learn from this and how this situation can possibly benefit you in the future. Sometimes the most horrific events in life can blossom into positive transformation.

- *Care for yourself.* Instead of binge-eating, indulging in excessive alcohol, and lying around feeling sorry for yourself, you can decide to care for yourself with a nutritious meal, enjoy a cup of relaxing tea, go for a walk, or meditate for a few minutes. Taking a restorative power nap can also produce wonderful benefits.

- *Accept your situation.* You don't always have control of the things that happen to you. Think of the things you do have control over and focus on them. You can control your emotions and how you react to events. You can manage your diet, who you hang with, your self-talk, your decisions, and your actions.

- *Remove yourself.* Remove yourself from negative people. Stay away from people who constantly complain and tend to drag you down with them. Shy away from situations that foster poor behavior. Find people and events that make you feel good and happy.

- *Remain in the present moment.* When experiencing tense times of crisis, it is always beneficial to practice mindfulness and various breathing techniques. Focusing your mind on the task at hand or on whatever you are doing at the moment helps bring stability into your awareness. Slowing your body and mind down during meditation will induce a state of clear and calm, and may provide insight into problem-solving.

- *Be the silent observer.* Practice observing problematic situations as if you were viewing them from outside yourself. Look at them from the perspective of the silent witness, just observing events as they occur. This approach may give rise to intuitive insights and solutions that may not have come to mind otherwise.

- *Honor yourself.* Give yourself a break, forgive yourself, know that you are not perfect and that you will make mistakes. Unfortunate, catastrophic things will happen to you too; things that you have no control over. Learn to relax and allow life to flow through you, knowing that things will work out in the long run. Love and care for yourself as if you were taking care of your little child.

- Find a local EMDR practitioner and move beyond your past emotional triggers. The treatments are reasonably priced and may only take several sessions to eliminate symptoms.

- Learn to tap. EFT tapping can produce immediate, positive results eliminating or reducing stress, anxiety, fear, pain, etc.

Resources

VeryWellMind: www.verywellmind.com. Search for the article "Stress, Chronic Stress, and Stress Relief."

American Psychological Association: www.apa.org. Search for the article "Coping with Stress."

Chopra Addiction and Wellness Center: www.chopratreatmentcenter.com. Search for the article "5 Simple Steps to Begin Healing from Emotional Trauma."

EMDR Institute Inc: www.emdr.com.

The Tapping Solution: www.thetappingsolution.com.

Reminder: You can find all live resource links on the author's website at AwakenMyPotential.com.

Chapter Ten

Integrity and Character

How To Develop It

Integrity can be defined as keeping to a standard of moral and ethical principles. But that's just a definition. More important is the question of how do we define the qualities of integrity and character within ourselves?

Each of us has in mind our own definition and expression of these qualities. As we are each unique; so are our expressions of integrity and character. The standards held by one person may be higher or lower than another's.

Integrity and character are two sides of the same coin.

Integrity is represented by being honest and having strong moral principles. It is the unwavering adherence to a strict moral and ethical code of honor and great character.

Character involves the combination of mental and moral qualities that distinguish a person, group, or thing from another. It differentiates the attributes of an individual, group, or category. It represents the core values that make them who they are.

Character is the code. Integrity is living according to that code.

A person of great character is one who presents himself in an open, sincere manner. One who always takes the honest approach no matter how much pressure they are encountering.

Some people maintain their integrity and character differently in business than they do in their personal lives. I once worked with a devout Christian who handed out religious pamphlets, held monthly meetings with a popular Bible distribution society, and often spoke of his Sunday and Wednesday church attendance. He openly shared his religious beliefs, and yet, I consistently observed him overtly lying to his customers to make automobile sales. Perhaps in his mind, he was merely doing business.

I'm not trying to judge him for his actions; I am certainly nowhere near perfect. However, I make every attempt to be honest in my business and personal lives. Yet, I would be lying if I claimed to be totally honest all the time. All, or at least most of us, lie at some time or another.

For example, how many times have you told someone their artwork, writing, hairdo, outfit, or creation of some sort was very nice when you really did not care for it at all? Even though you did not want to hurt their feelings, you were still lying. Is there a difference between a white or a black lie?

For me, a lie is a lie. I will make a sincere effort to refrain from comment or simply state that I appreciate their work/creation or mention it is "interesting." That is the safest way for me to avoid being dishonest.

I have lied about my past and present behaviors as well as mistakes to preserve my integrity as perceived by others. I am not proud of this, and I have to work consistently on being authentic and honest in all areas of my life. A client may provide me with improper paperwork and cause me a lot of extra work. They may apologize and I will reply that it is no problem at all when, in fact, it is. I don't want them to feel bad, so I lie. Instead, I could just tell them not to worry about it as this happens occasionally.

For some, I am sure expressing a high level of integrity is more difficult than for others. Some people express integrity easily. There are those whose lives seem to be effortless with business mistakes and personal missteps being few. They don't have to sacrifice their integrity for success as some will do.

What makes the difference is that they manage to maintain integrity in spite of their shortcomings. They don't allow failures or weaknesses to influence their lives to the point where they sacrifice their integrity.

We can develop habits that elevate our sense of integrity. Each time we find ourselves in a position that may compromise our trustworthiness, we can decide to do the right thing in spite of the opinions of others.

I am reminded of when a salesman I know double charged a customer for products they had purchased from him. He told me the customer had no idea and would probably never notice. I told him it did not matter that the customer did not realize it; the only thing that mattered was doing the right thing and refunding the overcharge, which he did promptly.

Even if integrity is most demanding, we can overcome the temptation to be dishonest by realizing the importance of being true to ourselves and others. Yes, at times, it is far easier to be dishonest than it is to be forthright. Each time we are dishonest, however, we weaken ourselves and become susceptible to the influence of negative, disempowering attitudes and beliefs.

Each time we are dishonest (and get away with it) it becomes easier to do so again. You overcharge a customer for some quick cash and the temptation to repeat it may recur almost immediately. It could even be easier the second time. This dishonest behavior settles within your mind and causes future guilt or remorse which can impede your forward progress.

Great character involves an enormous amount of authenticity and straightforward behavior. People of great character are rarely affected by the attitudes and behaviors of others. They understand that doing the right thing is always paramount to taking the easy path. Their distinctive mental and moral values lead them to make decisions that are in the best interest of themselves and others.

Those who struggle with character issues may find themselves commonly under stress. Dishonest behavior can lead to self-doubt and feelings of guilt or shame. It can deprive us of the freedom to exist in an environment of confidence and self-satisfaction.

When we are dishonest, we spend precious energy and sacrifice valuable space within our brain to hide our poor behavior and the feelings associated with it.

Do not beat yourself up if you struggle with being dishonest to others, or even yourself, at times. We are all human. The magazine, *Psychology Today,* cites studies by Dr. Bella DePaulo, former Professor of Psychology and current Project Scientist at the University of California, Santa Barbara. She states that people lie in *one in five* of their interactions. Not only do people lie to strangers, couples regularly deceive each other.

For example, her research showed that dating couples lie to each other about a third of the time. While that may be a disturbing figure, married couples were shown to do so with one in ten interactions.

Dr. DePaulo also found that while people seem to tell fewer of the "little" or "everyday" lies to loved ones, 64% of our serious lies ("deep betrayals of trust") do involve our closest relationship partners.

The behaviors displayed by these shocking study results can devastate loving, personal relationships as well as trusted business relationships.

I wonder if perhaps certain levels of integrity are inherited through our genes. Of course, I have no proof; this is my personal speculation. Regardless, I believe we should place ourselves in a position to foster trust and confidence in ourselves and others.

How can we do this? Consider the following solutions.

Solutions

- *Be honest with yourself.* We can fool ourselves into believing it is fine to tell white lies. Each time we allow ourselves to lie, it opens the doors for additional lies to surface with little regard for our conscience. It is better to remain silent at times than to speak an untruth.

- *Be honest with others.* Make every attempt to tell the truth in all circumstances. When our lies to others are discovered, we lose credibility and our personal relationships and status on the job suffer. We must accept responsibly for our actions and mistakes.

- *Be strong.* We must not succumb to the pressures of our peers, supervisors, society, or family to step beyond the boundary of truth. Even if we fail to "fit in" with the crowd, we should always honor our core values and beliefs. We must act congruently with the words we speak.

- *Be diligent.* Always work toward being the very best person you can be. Continually reassess your intentions and ask yourself if you are making the very best decisions that will benefit you and others while maintaining the highest level of integrity.

Resources

The Huffington Post (Huffpost): www.huffingtonpost.com. Search for the article "Character and Integrity at Work."

The Journal of Healthcare: www.jhconline.com. Search for the article "Leadership Strengths: Strong in Character & Integrity."

Success Magazine: www.success.com. Search for the article "9 Tips to Help You Strengthen Your Integrity."

Reminder: You can find all live resource links on the author's website at AwakenMyPotential.com.

Chapter Eleven

Beliefs—The Human Guidance System

Change Your Beliefs and Control Your Destiny

Earlier, we spoke briefly about the power of beliefs and how they affect our lives. Let's examine them more closely as they are one of the most powerful influences of our day-to-day living.

Beliefs guide us in virtually every decision we make. They hold the keys to our happiness and our misery. They lay the groundwork for our successes and our failures. They lead us in the direction of our hopes and our fears.

Our belief system is comprised of three categories: *adopted beliefs, indoctrinated beliefs,* and *intentional beliefs.*

Adopted beliefs are those that we choose to accept as truth. Most of our adopted belief were formulated during our childhood, either consciously or unconsciously. These beliefs were taught to us by our parents, friends, relatives, teachers, and religious leaders.

An example of an adopted belief would be that your mother told you only to eat bananas that were firm and had green on each end. All during your childhood, bananas that ripened to bright yellow with brown spots were discarded.

It is important to understand that, in most cases, these beliefs preceded our experiences. Because we accepted or adopted beliefs of others, our minds went about finding ways to prove these beliefs to be true.

When we adopt the beliefs of others, we invite experiences into our lives that confirm these beliefs. Think of a time, no matter at what point in your life, when you became interested in a particular model of a car you had never noticed before. Once this car was made known to you, many of these cars were brought into your awareness regularly. Previously, you had not observed this car, but now you see this model everywhere.

Let's return to our banana example. As a result of your adopted belief, your taste had become accustomed to the lesser ripe bananas, and you avoided the riper bananas altogether. Because you believed what your mother espoused, your experience confirmed yours and your mother's belief about bananas.

Later on suppose, in adulthood, a friend convinces you to try a riper banana and you find it to be delightful. Your belief now changes to accommodate your newly acquired taste for the fully ripened fruit.

An indoctrinated belief is one that is repeatedly drilled into your mind, usually with a negative consequence involved. One example might be that your religious leader continually admonishes you to attend church each Sunday or you will succumb to the evil ways of the world.

Out of fear, you attend church regularly. Any disobedience to this belief would cause you to slide into guilt and shame, abiding in an immoral world. Let's say later on in life, you find yourself preoccupied with changing jobs and moving from city to city. You realize at one point that you have not attended church in months.

At first, you panic, but then you come to an understanding that your heart has not changed. You feel the same peace you felt when you were attending church on a regular basis. You are not experiencing a wicked, sinful world. You now understand that your soul is pure, and you can navigate your life without the fear of disobedience invading your consciousness.

Now your belief has changed so that you don't feel you have to attend church "every" Sunday to enjoy your faith and to hold fast to your religious standards.

The third type of beliefs are intentional, deliberately created beliefs. What are they?

These are beliefs that *you decide* to create. They hold the keys to your hopes, successes, and happiness. Beliefs that you create are yours, and yours alone.

Adopted and indoctrinated beliefs are incredibly powerful. They can steer your life as firmly as your created beliefs (and may be even stronger at times). However, the ones you create place *you* in the driver's seat.

You will no longer be controlled by the generationally handed down or dogmatic beliefs of others. The beliefs you originate will guide you to the place of your dreams and not that of others.

There are three types of beliefs: *enabling beliefs, neutral beliefs, and disabling beliefs.* Each of these types can appear in any of the three categories: *adopted, indoctrinated,* or *intentional.*

Neutral beliefs are factually based, such as the sky is blue, water is wet, and feathers are light. They hold little or no power over us. They are just common knowledge, learned information. They do not impact our lives either positively or negatively.

Disabling beliefs are those that keep us at bay, the ones that control our lives in ways that are not conducive to living at will. Bosses are mean, relationships hurt, and mistakes are unacceptable are disabling beliefs that deprive us of joy and cause us to stumble.

Enabling beliefs empower us. They make us feel good and move us forward on the paths of *our* choosing. For example, I live in a peaceful world, my life is meaningful, I love the work I do.

We need not concern ourselves with neutral beliefs as they are of little importance. We naturally screen those out and pay no attention to them.

Our focus should be on the remaining two. First, we should strive to rid ourselves of as many disabling beliefs as we can. Second, we should create beliefs that enable us to reach our most significant potential.

A few years ago, I experienced a particularly memorable and inexplicable event. I participated in a mystifying firewalk ceremony in which I, mindfully, walked on 1,100 degree burning hardwood coals... three times!

Before walking the coals, my fellow participants and I spent the entire afternoon preparing mentally and physically. We bent six feet long rebars (3/8 inch thick steel rods) with the soft spot at the base of our throats. We broke target arrows in the same manner. We broke pine boards with our hands. Lastly, we walked with bare feet on broken glass from assorted bottles in a wide array of colors.

These were confidence-building exercises, masterfully crafted to encourage us participants to move forward in a confident, inspired, and fearless way. Each of the activities engendered moments of transformation that built upon themselves.

The very second my bare feet stepped onto the fiery coals, my life was transformed. It was a moment like no other in my entire life. I felt unstoppable, as though no obstacles could impede my path. The heat rising from the charcoals was intense, and yet somehow it did not even singe the hair on my legs.

It took about five or six steps to traverse the fifteen or more feet of hot coals. Each step was a miraculous event, and I felt inspired to continue on and trek the fire two more times.

It was my enabling belief that I would not be affected by the burning coals that motivated me to continue. It was my enabling belief that prevented my feet from being burned and blistered. It was my enabling belief that allowed me to move beyond my preconceived ideas of limitation.

No one wants to look back on their life with regret. No one wants to be a failure. When our goals are established within the ego-mind, we set ourselves up for ultimate failure.

We should specify goals that are not self-serving, but ones that meet our desires in ways that do not infringe upon the wellbeing of others.

Ego-centric is about me. Ethno-centric is about my group. World-centric is about my world. Cosmo-centric is about all of life. May our goals and intentions be entrenched in a cosmo-centric manner.

Consider your beliefs, and challenge those that are not serving you well. Your enabling and disabling beliefs will consistently thrust you toward success or failure in many areas of your life as you allow.

Eliminating disabling beliefs before you attempt setting goals can make the difference between achievement and nonfulfillment. Remember, beliefs control your destiny. Change your beliefs, and you will likely change your destiny.

Solutions

- Understand the importance of beliefs and how they impact your life and direct your path.

- Discover beliefs that may be holding you back and eliminate them.

- Create new beliefs that empower you to move toward your goals.

- Write down on paper or your smart device your goals and intentions. Seeing is believing.

- Write your intentions in the present tense as if they have already been achieved.

- Vividly visualize your goal. See it within your mind and feel it within your body as if it was actually happening at that moment with all sights, sounds, and scents. Experience the deep emotions attached to it and focus on that part of you that wants to achieve the goal.

Resources

Forbes: www.forbes.com. Search for the article "Forget Positive Thinking: This Is How To Actually Change Negative Thoughts For Success."

CNBC: www.cnbc.com. Search for the article "This Simple Method Is Used by Bill Gates, Larry Page and Even Bono to Tackle Their Biggest Goals."

Entrepreneur: www.entrepreneur.com. Search for the article "6 Tips for Goal-Setting That, Trust Me, They Don't Teach You in College."

Reminder: You can find all live resource links on the author's website at AwakenMyPotential.com.

Chapter Twelve

Affirmations

They Can Make a Believer Out of You

Many self-help authors, including Tony Robbins, suggest using positive affirmations to solidify desired beliefs. I am a firm believer of this. I have used affirmations for many years and have found the effects to be quite helpful at times.

But there is a trick to using affirmations in a way that enables personal change. Affirmations are not supportive if you do not use good visualization skills to supplement them. For instance, if you make the affirmation, "I am a great speed-reader," you must visualize yourself reading rapidly.

This visualization should be done in a quiet setting with all of your attention on "experiencing" being a speed-reader. Within your mind, see yourself speed-reading, experience it as if it was really happening, feel what it feels like to perform this task, and believe that it is in the process of development.

Affirmations must be initiated regularly, too. Conducting a visualization session one time will more than likely not be enough to bring the affirmation to fruition. It is in repetition that mastery is created. Some may believe that one time is all it takes and achievement will ensue. This may very well happen for the one in a million who attempt this, but the vast majority will not realize the anticipated results.

Keep in mind, affirmations possess more power when there is a sincere intention and intense emotion consistently involved. Just stating the affirmation, which should be spoken out loud, will have little or no effect. There has to be a compelling meaning with an emotional connection.

Repetition and connection are the reasons why advertisers bombard us repeatedly with the same television or radio commercials. Have you ever noticed how most commercials show a physically beautiful person enjoying their product or service? They also display how wonderful life would be for you in ideal surroundings and situations.

They want you to experience, in your mind, how you would feel owning their product. They want you to see how fit and healthy, happy and content, successful and wealthy, and beautiful and poised you will look having their product or service. Good advertisers know how to appeal to your desires and motivate you to purchase from them. Advertising is powerful!

Let's talk about the Law of Attraction for a moment. The Law of Attraction states that when you ask for what you want and believe with unwavering faith that it is yours, then you will receive it.

For instance, say you have a strong desire to be a speed-reader and you believe that you are becoming one. This is a good start, but in order to receive it you must put forth effort and action to enable the process. It is essential for you to practice speed-reading to acquire the skill, even if that practice is only within your mind as a mental rehearsal. If you want to be an attorney-at-law, you had better attend law school and educate yourself in the ways of your specific field to be successful. Just asking and believing will not place a law degree in your lap.

There is always *action* that must be taken to achieve results. Yes, ask to become a lawyer, believe that you are one, and receive it as if it was done. Vivid affirmations should enhance this process, but please, take the action steps necessary to ensure your success. Action is of utmost importance in the Law of Attraction and is the often missing final step.

Anticipating the best outcome is always optimal. However, you have to be realistic to some extent in most situations. The old axiom, "expect the best, plan for the worst" does have merit. I am not being negative here, just real. It is always in your best interest to be prepared for outcomes that you may not have anticipated.

Consider this example as illustration. Let's pretend you set a goal to retire five years from now but you fail to create an alternate plan in case some unforeseen event occurs that negatively impinges on your goal. What might happen then if, two months prior to your scheduled retirement, the economy slips into recession and you cannot afford to retire?

Had you originally formulated an alternate plan of action, you would now find yourself in a position to adjust your goal quickly. Your back-up plan could have been to build a financial safety net to support you long enough while you seek employment once more.

In Deepak Chopra's book, *The Seven Spiritual Laws of Success*, he addresses this issue. One of his affirmations under his fifth law, Law of Intention and Desire, states "I surrender my list of intentions and desires to the Universe, trusting that things will go according to the Divine plan, knowing that it may not always seem to go my way."

Yes, trust with all your heart that things will go your way, but understand that there is a possibility things may not evolve the way you anticipate.

Affirmations can add elements of enhancement to any goal. An example would be, "I feel satisfied retiring on September 30, 2___." Always state your affirmation and a goal in the present as if you have already achieved them. This way, the mind begins to accept it as a reality when the affirmation is repeated again and again.

Repetition is the key. Anything you practice over and over again will assist you in solidifying the outcome. Affirmations can promote motivation to stay on course. They can also assist your mind in building new neural pathways.

As for immediate results, the proof will be in your findings. Affirmations may become a long-term process. Don't get discouraged if you do not realize instant achievement. You may want to consider creating a belief that your affirmations are working quickly and effectively.

Also, you should consider multiple affirmations for each goal. For instance, based on the previous example regarding retirement, you could create the following additional affirmations:

- "I feel wonderful promoting good health in my retirement by exercising every day."

- "I experience gratitude, knowing that I am managing my retirement spending attentively."

- "I feel rewarded and blessed, being able to do the things I want to do in my retirement."

- "I am worthy of retirement and it feels great!"

Concerning the last affirmation above, you must understand what being "worthy" means to you. Know that you deserve your retirement due to all your years of hard work and dedication. Recognize that retirement is your reward and you are entitled to it. Experience the feeling you get once you are fully engaged with this knowledge.

Next, for it to fully sink in, feel what that truly feels like with your emotional self. Ignore the impulse to think about it. Just feel it! Become aware of the place these feelings are held in your body. Zero in on it and hold your attention there for a moment or two. Savor this moment and remember how good it feels. You can return to this state of mind anytime you wish, and the more often, the better.

Solutions

- Search yourself that you are not holding negative affirmations, such as "I am not smart" or "I am never going to be good at this." Change those into positive affirmations instead.

- Write your intentions in present tense as if they have already been achieved.

- Create affirmations as your goals and repeat them often. Remember, affirmations that you do not believe will have no lasting effects. Your subconscious mind will not accept them as reality.

- Vividly visualize your goal. See it within your mind and feel it within your body as if it was actually happening at that moment with all the sights, sounds, and scents. Experience the deep emotions attached to it and focus on that part of you that wants to achieve the goal.

- Maintain optimism and allow things to unfold as they will rather than attempting to force them into existence. You can change emotions, feelings, and mental states, but you cannot improve outcomes or events once they have occurred.

Resources

Dr. Joe Vitale: wwwmrfire.com or www.joevitale.com. Joe is one of the stars in the hit movie, The Secret. He is a prolific author, mentor, motivational speaker, songwriter, and musician. He offers something for everyone relating to personal development.

Forbes: www.forbes.com. Search for the article "Forget Positive Thinking: This Is How To Actually Change Negative Thoughts For Success."

CNBC: www.cnbc.com. Search for the article "This Simple Method Is Used by Bill Gates, Larry Page, and Even Bono to Tackle Their Biggest Goals."

Entrepreneur: www.entrepreneur.com. Search for the article "6 Tips for Goal-Setting That, Trust Me, They Don't Teach You in College."

Reminder: You can find all live resource links on the author's website at AwakenMyPotential.com.

Chapter Thirteen

Intuition

Enable Your Genius Within

Intuition is the faculty of acquiring direct knowledge without rational evidence. Many people make reference to this as the sixth sense. There is no interference with thought, only an instinct, a gut feeling, or second sight. Science describes this as unconscious reasoning.

Intuitive impulses may surface anytime and can be experienced viscerally. Some people only recognize these impulses on rare occasions; others glimpse these feelings many times each day. These impulses may be formed from our knowledge bank or our past experiences. They are always present, waiting to be noticed and utilized.

Intuition can manifest itself in various ways. Your heart rate might increase, you may feel clammy or sweaty, you may feel a tingly sensation viscerally, or you might feel a sudden shift in your awareness. There are other ways as well. Each individual will experience the impression of intuition differently.

Our ability to encounter these instincts largely depends on our states of mind. When we are unhappy or under a great deal of stress, we may ignore these impulses or not recognize them at all. If we are preoccupied with negative thoughts of our current situation or we are mentally living in the past or future, we can miss opportunities to allow our intuition to guide us.

Still, it is up to us to perceive an intuitive impulse and act upon it. In whatever ways intuition strikes us, we may be far more likely to recognize it when we keep a clear, open mind.

Why is it so vital for us to encounter and act upon our intuitive impulses?

Intuition may be the purest form of knowledge emanating directly from the source of consciousness or universal information. It stems from the source of all that is. You may reference this source as Collective or Cosmic Consciousness, Source, Infinite Mind, God, Universe, God of your heart, Higher Self, Spirit, Divine Matrix, etc.

It is advantageous for us to be guided by our intuition rather than our thinking brains. Brains and minds are entirely different things. Brains are organs within the body, and the mind is in and of everything. It is not contained within the body. It has no boundaries and is not limited to or contained within any space.

Our brains are merely computers, though very sophisticated computer systems. Mind, however, encompasses the entire body and beyond. When we utilize intuition, we tap into mind, the source of all that is—the field, infinite intelligence, universal mind, super consciousness, however you wish to refer to it.

This is the center of your being. It is the most crucial element of your life. If you fail to connect and explore this region, you are missing out on opportunities to expand, grow, and mature into your highest potential.

Steve Jobs of Apple fame referenced intuition as being more powerful than intellect. However you perceive it, intuition can guide us through the most challenging times of our lives. Even in the most difficult of situations, intuition can assist us in making decisions that are the most appropriate.

Think on this illustration. One morning, while getting her child ready for school, a mother receives an impression of danger involving her child. She does not understand the perception but decides to keep her child home from school that day.

Later that afternoon, she sees a news report of a mass shooting at her child's school. How could she have known? Why did she believe this impulse was a warning of some sort?

She knew, at some level, that this was a truth radiating from within (or maybe from her perspective or from outside of her). She acted upon it because she believed this to be wisdom from her Higher Self. Some people might attribute this gut feeling as an inspiration from God which could, essentially, be the same thing.

Intuition is not experienced in the thinking mind but rather in our feelings. We *feel* when the time is right. We *feel* when we are needed the most. We *feel* when we must change something about ourselves.

It is in consciousness that we feel. The Spirit or God does not communicate with us in our thoughts. Our *feelings* sense this urging, this beckoning. We transform these feelings into thoughts and describe them with our minds based on our belief system and outlook on life. When our minds are cluttered with over-thinking and worry, we suppress the urges of our deepest, innate feelings.

Operating in "feel mode" should be a high priority. When we are feeling, we are listening to the higher dictates of our consciousness.

We need to know when we should be thinking or listening. When we are thinking, we are "doing." When we are feeling, we are "non-doing." In doing the thinking, we are controlling the situation in rational terms. This is perfectly normal in many situations.

However, when people allow their feelings to prevail, providing that they are in alignment with their Higher Selves and their motives are pure, then they will be in a better position to receive direct input. They will obtain the correct information to help them make the very best decision at that time.

Acting upon intuitive impulses requires a clear mind and an open heart. It is necessary to free yourself from the events occurring around you so you can listen closely and observe the impulses at hand. This means to remove yourself from the situation for a moment and allow your senses to detect information that may be otherwise ignored.

Let's say you are working on an assembly line with very loud equipment while wearing noise-canceling earphones. You don't notice that your fellow employee, a good friend, is scuffling right next to you with another employee who is a bully. The brawl lasts a couple of minutes, and your friend becomes injured. There is no guarantee that you would have noticed the fight had you been making avail of your intuition. It does stand to reason that you could have been in a position to sense the situation. If you had been more aware of your feelings, you might have been able to intervene appropriately.

I understand that intuition plays a more prominent role in life for some over others. Some people are too preoccupied with their current situation or are just not in touch with that part of themselves. Some are consistently piloted by intuition in ways that I wish I could experience.

Most of us have to take time, as often as we can, to deliberately listen and be aware of our surroundings. We can expand our senses and enhance our awareness with practice. There are many avenues to explore to do this. In my case, martial arts helped me greatly to develop skills in these areas.

I used to think some people were gifted with superior intuition. That may very well be true. However, I think it is possible for anyone to develop a higher level of intuition. Intuition permeates the world we live in. It is intrinsic to the lives we lead. Accessing and developing intuition is essential to living more productive, pleasurable, and self-directed lives. Employ the following solutions to lead you in the right direction.

Solutions

- Get out of your head and get into your gut more often. Balance your rational brain with your feeling mind. When you catch yourself over-analyzing, transition into observing your feelings.

- Develop your intuition. Feel your way into situations and explore possibilities while being the silent witness. This is where you observe without judgment and allow unlimited mind to intercede with unimpeded flow.

- Listen carefully to that subtle urging within. Does an image come to mind? Do you hear words spoken in your mind? Do you feel sensations in a specific location in your body?

- When faced with choices, consider each outcome and observe your feelings about them. One should feel better or more comfortable than another. You may receive the slightest impression directing you toward the best choice.

- Practice mindfulness by paying attention to your current experience in a non-judgmental way. Observe your surroundings and interactions with others in a more in-depth, more open manner.

- Meditate as often as you can. Find a quiet place where you will be completely undisturbed and take time (even if it is only ten minutes) to relax and allow things to be just as they are. Discover a meditation style you feel comfortable with and make it your daily practice. This will improve your connection to intuition.

- Dismiss negative emotions. Being upset, angry, or feeling out of sorts can interfere with intuitive impulses. Recover as quickly as you can from negative situations and return to a clear mind and open heart.

- Quiet your mind. Intuition most commonly arises from a quiet mind. The more times you quiet your mind during the day, even if only for a moment or two, the more opportunities you will have to experience these impulses.

- Act upon your intuitive impulses. Feel your way through situations. Feel, listen, and then act. Don't worry about making the wrong decision. Just be open and aware, observing the information that becomes available to you.

Resources

Psychology Today: www.psychologytoday.com. Search for the article "Here's a Quick Way to Develop Your Intuition."

Oprah: www.oprah.com. Search for the article "The Science of Intuition: An Eye-Opening Guide to Your Sixth Sense."

HeartMath: www.heartmath.com. Search for the article "Solution for Developing Your Intuition."

Reminder: You can find all live resource links on the author's website at AwakenMyPotential.com.

Chapter Fourteen

Consciousness and the Brain

Access Your Super Powers

You hear it all the time: "connect with your consciousness," "explore your consciousness." Exactly, what is consciousness? No one knows! So, this chapter will not be a detailed study of all the theories regarding consciousness. Instead, I will attempt to convey a straightforward approach to navigating states of consciousness to your benefit.

Consciousness can be considered as pure awareness, infinite information, unlimited potential, an unlimited mind, etc. There may be many levels of consciousness, or mind, that we move into throughout each day.

Many scientists believe consciousness resides in the physical realm, i.e., located within the brain. Others believe it is non-local, instead being in and of everything, permeating all life on our planet while comprising the whole of the universe. Brain waves and consciousness are interrelated and operate synchronistically so we can experience our reality.

I'll now share with you some dimensions of consciousness so you can understand how important they are and how you can observe and then elevate your level of being.

For simplicity, we'll divide consciousness into only three basic categories—Dimension One: Higher; Dimension Two: Middle; and Dimension Three: Lower. There are sub-categories in each level as well. These sub-categories are only a modest representation of all the possibilities.

Dimension One: Super/Elevated Consciousness

Cognition: unsullied knowing, perception.

Being: pure awareness/beingness, silent witness, potentiality, source.

Observing: using the mind deliberately, free attention, watching, quiet mind.

165

Intuiting: feeling, listening within.

Imagining: using imagination deliberately, creating, employing intentions, conceptualizing.

Allowing: non-judgmental, benevolent, peaceful, loving, happy, free to be who you are.

Dimension Two: Working/Functional

Thinking: analyzing, studying.

Remembering: recreating the past, reliving prior events, fixed attention, anticipating what to say or do next.

Autopilot: operating on autopilot, allowing the mind to wander and imagine without deliberate intention (daydreaming), not being fully present.

Dimension Three: Impaired/Unconscious

Monkey Mind: restless, distracted, ego-based, inner critic, unrestrained talking and verbal responses.

Reacting: engaging the ego, negative carnal tendencies, pride, anger, jealousy, emotional outbursts.

Self-indulgence: narcissistic, selfishness, criminal behavior, hoarding, taking advantage of others.

Psychotic: mental illness, insanity.

Unconscious: Unawake, asleep.

Throughout each day, we find ourselves migrating from one dimension (level) to another moment by moment. Obviously, it would serve us well to operate in Dimensions One and Two the vast majority of the time, with the exception of sleep. (There is not much we can alter during times of sleep. This is where our bodies recuperate and regenerate from the day's activities.) Even though we may migrate from one dimension to another moment by moment, crossing the threshold into Dimension One as often as possible is ideal.

Our brainwave functions have a massive impact on how we adjust and adapt to our external and internal environments. The brain operates within several levels of brainwaves. There are five basic brainwaves. (Other brainwaves have been detected, but we will concentrate on the basics.) Keep in mind, there is a difference of opinions in the scientific arena regarding the exact levels of Hertz. The standard measurement of Hertz frequencies is one cycle per second.

Brain Sync, a brainwave technology company, describes the five brainwave functions as follows.

Gamma: inspiration, higher learning, focus.

Gamma waves are the fastest of the brainwave frequencies and signify the highest state of focus possible. They are associated with peak concentration and are the brain's optimal frequency for cognitive functioning. Nobel prize-winning scientist, Sir Francis Crick, believes that the 40Hz frequency may be the key to the act of cognition. (The variable range is 38-42Hz.)

Beta: alertness, concentration, cognition.

In Beta, you are wide-awake and alert. Your mind is sharp, focused. It makes connections quickly, easily, and you're primed to do work that requires your full attention. In the Beta state, neurons fire abundantly, in rapid succession, helping you achieve peak performance. New ideas and solutions to problems flash like lightning into your mind. (The variable range is 12-40Hz.)

Alpha: relaxation, visualization, creativity.

The Alpha state is an intensely pleasurable and relaxed state of consciousness essential to stress reduction and high levels of creativity. Artists, musicians, and athletes are prolific alpha producers. So are intuitive persons. Alpha researcher Joe Kamiya says, "Its pleasure may come from the fact that alpha represents something like letting go of anxieties." (The variable range is 8-12Hz.)

Theta: meditation, intuition, memory.

Theta is one of the more elusive and extraordinary brain states you can explore. It is also known as the twilight state, which you typically only experience fleetingly upon waking or drifting off to sleep. Theta is the brain state where magic happens in the crucible of your own neurological activity. For most, being able to enter the dreamlike Theta state without falling asleep takes meditation practice. (The variable range is 3-8Hz.)

Delta: healing, sleep, detached awareness.

In the Delta state, you are sound asleep. Delta waves are the slowest of all the five brainwave frequencies and range between 0-4 Hz. Slow Wave Sleep, or SWS, is the deepest of sleep states, and it plays a vital role in health and well-being. During this phase of the sleep cycle, the brain begins producing very slow, large Delta waves. (The variable range is 0-4Hz.)

All of these brainwaves can be observed in EEGs (electroencephalograms) operating simultaneously as a symphony of waves, although, one of these five will dominate at any given moment. This is why we experience psychological and physiological changes during the day.

It is helpful to recognize in what state of mind and brainwave dimensions we are operating in during our waking times. If we are feeling very relaxed and lethargic or sleepy, residing in the Alpha or Theta state, and have an important task to perform that requires a great deal of mental clarity and acuity, then we may want to ratchet up our brainwave level a notch or two into the Gamma or Beta states.

If your mind is racing and reliving your day's experiences at bedtime, then you will want to slow your brainwaves down into Alpha to induce a very relaxed state in preparation for ascension into Theta and Delta for sleep.

Too much Beta or Gamma can result in scattered, undisciplined, overactive thinking. Behavioral control deteriorates as the hyperactive brain releases chemicals that interfere with and cloud thinking processes. It's like forcing your way into an overcrowded subway car. There's too much going on in there!

Too much Theta or Delta and you may find yourself slumped over at your desk wondering how you will manage to complete your tasks. Do you recognize this as a need for caffeine? Stimulants can be effective, but there are drawbacks such as dependency, ease of overuse, unhealthy chemicals and additives, and costs.

If we can learn to control our brainwaves, we can operate in higher states of mind. This can be accomplished with breathing techniques, stretching, exercising, music, sound wave technology, and visualization. I will point you in the right direction in the Solutions section.

Higher states of mind lead to a more fulfilled sense of being. Mastering techniques of brainwave level transitions allow us to control our environment and optimize our mental and emotional states. It enables us to perform tasks and interactions with others at higher levels.

Elevated levels of consciousness can transform situations of stress and conflict into calm, relaxed positions of allowing and wellbeing. The capacity to engage life to the degree that a sense of total and complete oneness occurs is crucial.

Feeling that you are an integral piece of the whole of humanity and that you are connected intrinsically at every level is essential to an expanded sense of consciousness. This is where the heart of living truly exists. It is the interstice between the thoughts, the space between the breaths, the quiet moments of being.

As for most things learned, transitioning through brainwave states takes practice. However, when we observe how beneficial it is to change states of being on demand, we will find ourselves desiring it as it leads to greater efficiency.

Merely becoming aware of brainwave activity and how it affects our state of mind and physiology is enough to accelerate the process of development.

Besides the traditional eastern approaches of yoga and meditation to bring brainwaves into balance, there are some more modern methods available, such as neurofeedback and entrainment which we will discuss in the next chapter.

Solutions

- Make an intention to align yourself with Dimension One consciousness. This is where your highest potential exists. You use your mind quietly but deliberately.

- Become aware of your brainwave states. If you are too high in Gamma waves and your desire is to relax, then shift your attention to a lower frequency. To do this, breathe slowly and deeply to the count of eight and then exhale to the same count for a few minutes to induce a state of calm. Conversely, if you are feeling sleepy or lethargic, you can place your tongue on the roof of your mouth and breath rapidly in and out through your nose for a moment or two. Try it for twenty or thirty seconds at first and work your way up to a minute with three consecutive sessions. This will increase oxygen to your brain and escalate your energy and cognitive abilities.

- Resist engaging the ego and the monkey mind. The monkey mind prefers talking excessively as opposed to listening. It gets distracted easily and likes to criticize your every move. It is restless and self-indulgent. Listen to others patiently and empathetically. Observe your behavior with others as if you were on the outside looking in.

- Control your attention. Constantly place your attention in the present moment. Bring yourself back to the now with deliberate intention over and over again. Take advantage of Dimension Two: Working/Functional Consciousness by being fully present in the moment with the task at hand.

- Develop intuition. Feel your way into situations and explore possibilities while being the silent witness. This is where you observe without judgment and allow unlimited mind to intercede with unimpeded flow.

- Mimic Behavioral Targeting which is a marketing/advertising campaign technique. Here is an example of how this targeting works. While on the internet, you shop for a product that interests you but you don't make a purchase. Later, when you return to your shopping or web surfing activities, you see advertisements for the very product you clicked on earlier. Your shopping behavior has been targeted.

Mimic this behavior by becoming aware of the multitude of opportunities to change your states of mind. You can practice by deciding to relax into Alpha or raise your energy into Beta each time you see a specific color or a certain item (such as a hat), hear a phone ring, open a door, or anything that works for you.

Resources

Brain Sync: www.brainsync.com. Learn more about brainwave technology plus gain access to sound wave technology and guided meditations. Allow the sounds to meditate you.

Conscious Lifestyle Magazine: www.consciouslifestylemag.com. Search for the article "The Six Levels of Higher Consciousness: How to Make the Shift."

Deepak Chopra: www.sfgate.com. Search for the article "Can There Be a Science of Consciousness?"

Mindvalley: www.mindvalley.com. Founder, Vishen Lakhiani, has many excellent programs available for everyone involving business, personal, mind, health, and spirit.

Reminder: You can find all live resource links on the author's website at AwakenMyPotential.com.

Chapter Fifteen

Neurofeedback & Brainwave Entrainment

Make Your Brain Work Better For You

This may sound a little space-age, but let me assure you it is not. Neurofeedback is a proven, scientific technique that has been used for behavior modification with great results.

Neurofeedback essentially compares what your brain is doing verses what you would prefer your brain to be doing. Here is how it operates. Sensors are attached to the scalp that measure and monitor brain activity. Brain analysis software then identifies specific activities of symptomatic behaviors.

Next, a visual screen displays rewards, such as in a video game, when desired brainwave levels are attained. The process enables participants to learn how to control their brainwave activity based on the feedback received.

This awareness creates an increase in neuroplasticity, which is the change in brain structure and organization as we learn, experience, mature, and adapt to our ever-changing world.

Neural pathways, the connections within the brain, evolve steadily, becoming stronger or weaker depending on the brain's use. For example, aging can take its toll on these neural pathways as the brain can lose some of its plasticity. Also, if we become rigid and fixed in our ways and limit learning and perception, then our brains can lose mass and effectiveness. Younger brains, conversely, are more plastic and have a higher propensity for change.

Brainwave Entrainment

Brainwave entrainment is used to guide the brain into specific states such as relaxation, meditation, enhanced focus and concentration, trance, or sleep. Entrainment can assist those who have difficulties in attaining desired states of mind. It works as an autopilot, and can be easily accessed by almost everyone.

Brainwave entrainment stimulates the brain into entering specific states by utilizing light, sound pulsing, or electromagnetic fields. The brain responds to the pulsing sound beats or light flashes and is able to follow these stimuli and entrain itself into desired brainwave frequencies.

Remember, your dominant brainwave frequency fluctuates during the day, but that doesn't mean you are at your brain's mercy. For example, you may be operating in Beta and wish to slow down into Alpha. That's a perfect time to apply brain entrainment, thus putting you in control. You can synchronize your brain with the external stimulus of sound wave technology and binaural beats to create more desirable cortical responses befitting your desired mental state, which in our example is calmness.

Binaural beats therapy, an increasingly used method of brain entrainment, is a fascinating form of sound wave technology. Headphones are required as two different frequencies are employed, one in each ear. The left ear could be listening to 200Hz while the right ear hears 210Hz. This results in a perception of a binaural beat of 10Hz (the difference between 210Hz and 200Hz), a frequency within the relaxed, receptive Alpha range being experienced as one tone.

Binaural audio technology is widely available at low or no cost. You can find many smartphone apps and YouTube videos you can listen to with a good set of headphones, although CD's may be a better option for a purer sound. There are many options of binaural beats to choose from relating to various conditions you may be experiencing such as pain, anxiety, or frustration.

I have found brainwave entrainment to be beneficial to me in reading, writing, and studying. If you are not the type to sit in quiet contemplation for a specified duration as meditation requires, then sound wave therapy may work well for you.

One advantage to sound wave therapy is that it can be done while you are working. Right now, I am using my smartphone with earbuds to listen to binaural beats while writing this book. It drowns out the distractions around me and allows me to focus my attention on my work while operating in a relaxed, yet amazingly alert state.

Just be sure not to over-stimulate your brain. It may be favorable to begin with short, three to fifteen minute sessions. Brainworksneurotherapy.com warns of possible dangers of brainwave entrainment. "Do not use brainwave entrainment if you are prone to seizures (or if you're pregnant, in case you are prone to seizures and unaware of it). Take extra caution if under 26 years of age, as the brain is still developing and is more sensitive."

Solutions

- Experiment cautiously with brainwave entrainment. Search YouTube for "brainwave frequency" and add the Hertz you desire. There are many frequencies and binaural beat videos available. Plug in your headphones and give it a try. You need not watch the video, although the scenes are usually quite pleasant.

- Following the general guidelines provided by Brainworksneurotherapy.com will significantly limit your risk of discomfort.

> Don't overdo it; most cases side-effects come after overuse. A fifteen-minute session is sufficient to begin (or three to five minutes if you're using audio visual entrainment). Everyone reacts differently, and you will need to determine your sensitivity before jumping in full force.

> If you experience increased anxiety, convulsions, overwhelming subconscious images, nausea, headaches, dizziness, or increased heartbeat, discontinue use immediately and permanently.

Do not use brainwave entrainment if you have any brainwave hyper-arousal or instability symptoms.

Resources

iAwake Technologies: www.iawaketechnologies.com. Access brainwave and biofield entrainment with sophisticated technologies and consciousness enhancing tools.

Mindvalley: www.mindvalley.com. Founder, Vishen Lakhiani, has many excellent programs available for everyone involving business, personal, mind, health, and spirit.

Brain Sync: www.brainsync.com. Learn more about brainwave technology plus gain access to sound wave technology and guided meditations. Allow the sounds to meditate you.

Brainworks: www.brainworksneurotherapy.com. You can discover brain training techniques.

Reminder: You can find all live resource links on the author's website at AwakenMyPotential.com.

Chapter Sixteen

Visualization, Meditation, and Yoga

How To Effect Massive Change

Once thought of as the providence of Eastern medicine, visualization, meditation, and yoga have now become mainstream practices. All three, whether used alone or in conjunction, offer powerful, life-changing benefits.

As we learn to alter the conditions of our state of mind through these three techniques, we can modify habitual patterns of mental activity and emotional behaviors.

Visualization

Visualization of desired material objects, situations, relationships, events, or physical or mental conditions can support achievement. Visualization skills easily can be developed and enhanced with practice. They are typically applied during quiet times of relaxation or meditation in the Alpha state.

When you vividly create within your mind the desired outcome while in Alpha, your chances of success are multiplied. Overall, it is difficult for the mind to rationalize the difference between what is vividly imagined and what is actually experienced.

A typical visualization session is when you create a movie within your mind. If you want to buy a car that you have dreamed about owning, you make a mental movie of this car with you behind the wheel. You will want to experience, vividly within your mind, how it feels to drive it and operate all of the special features that you love.

An important element of visualization is to accompany the visuals with the associated feelings. How do you feel driving your new dream car?

Listening to music can enhance your visualization process. Music of various types can produce swift alterations to moods and energy levels. For example, hard driving rock and roll and up-tempo pop can invite more Gamma and Beta functioning to help you move forward with high energy workouts and mental or physical tasks.

Contrary to that, soothing symphonic, spa, or meditation music can induce states of Alpha and Delta to relax your mind and body. This will assist you in unwinding from your day, clearing your mind, preparing for sleep, or practicing meditation.

Choose the appropriate music for your visualization session, or simply experience silence.

Meditation

Meditation may be the optimal choice for those considering improved brainwave usage and development. Meditation is a primary practice for cultivating positive transformations in consciousness. It can create fundamental shifts in your outlook and states of being that affect every aspect of your life.

Some of my most treasured experiences have been during meditation. My skills have progressed to the point where my imagination is so vivid at times that it is difficult to distinguish it from waking, collective reality.

At times, I can create incredible, sacred moments of profound peace and clarity. Ideas, inspirations, answers to issues, all come to life and provide a deep sense of oneness and knowing.

Your capacity to engage life in more positive, meaningful ways is enhanced through the meditative experience of an interconnected whole and self-transcendence. It is a pathway into awakening and liberation from an inhibited sense of functioning. The role you play in life may become more free, expansive, and intuitive as the "you" you are in meditation becomes the "you" you are in daily living.

Meditation is known to improve cognitive stability, regulate and stabilize emotional responses, and ameliorate physical wellbeing. It retrains the brain to adapt more readily to the onslaught of negative, stressful events that life hurls at us on a regular basis.

As we learn to alter the conditions of our states of mind, we can modify particular habitual patterns of mental activity and emotional behaviors.

Recent discoveries in neurobiology have unearthed an incredible potential for change in the brain's operational systems. The brain's plasticity accommodates for modification of priorly believed fixed personality traits, such as moods and dispositions.

Experienced meditators seem to have more activity in the left frontal lobe of the brain which is associated with experiencing positive emotions, such as pleasure, happiness, and equanimity. These individuals display increases in psychological stability, improved mental clarity, reductions in symptoms of illness, immunological stimulation, and hormonal functioning.

An article by the Mayo Clinic staff cites the following: "When you meditate, you may clear away the information overload that builds up every day and contributes to your stress." The list of the emotional benefits of meditation is growing steadily as research and experimentation are verified. Currently, the noted benefits include:

- Gaining a new perspective on stressful situations.
- Building skills to manage your stress.
- Increasing self-awareness.
- Focusing on the present.
- Reducing negative emotions.
- Increasing imagination and creativity.
- Increasing patience and tolerance.

I have a natural tendency of being hyperactive and to overthink situations. Meditation helps calm my mind, relax my body, and think more clearly. It assists me in making decisions that are more intuitively centered.

Meditation might also be useful if you have a medical condition, especially one worsened by stress. A growing body of scientific research supports the health benefits of meditation. It's been proven that meditation may help people manage symptoms of conditions, such as:

- Anxiety
- Asthma
- Cancer
- Chronic pain
- Depression
- Heart disease
- High blood pressure
- Irritable bowel syndrome
- Sleep problems
- Tension headaches

Meditation is one of the least expensive treatments available today. The only requirements are small investments of time and dedication to the practice. You won't need the internet, devices of any kind, or your hard-earned dollars.

Yoga

Yoga is a means by which one can unite the mind, body, and spirit. It can combine exercise, breathwork, and meditation to promote better health and emotional wellbeing. Many modern yoga styles focus on physical aspects while more traditional styles incorporate mindfulness, meditation, and spiritual development.

Yoga has been proven through a host of studies to reduce stress, foster mental clarity and calmness, and engender emotional stability. The physical advantages are numerous, including improved posture and balance, digestion, oxygenation and circulation of the bloodstream, increased energy, flexibility, stamina, and self-discipline.

Yoga gently urges us inward to unconditionally listen, feel, and experience the body and the breath in the very moment of practice. During a session, we notice there is a beginning, a duration, and an ending, which helps us relate to current problems and past trauma in the same way.

According to Harvard Medical School's *Harvard Mental Health Letter* (updated 2018): "But for many patients dealing with depression, anxiety, or stress, yoga may be a very appealing way to better manage symptoms. Indeed, the scientific study of yoga demonstrates that mental and physical health are not just closely allied, but are essentially equivalent. The evidence is growing that yoga practice is a relatively low-risk, high-yield approach to improving overall health."

Almost anyone can benefit from yoga in a multitude of ways. Conduct some basic research and discover a method that works best for you. There are many styles designed to meet your needs and desires. Local community centers often provide lessons for little or no charge. There are yoga studios worldwide along with video programs available for the beginner and the advanced student.

Whenever a couple of weeks go by without practicing yoga, my body reminds me that it is time. Aches and pains increase, and I become aware that I have neglected my body. Pain and discomfort in my neck and back due to a former auto accident resurface, and I dutifully return to my routine for immediate relief A short session, even if it is alone by myself, brings my mind and body back into alignment.

Solutions

- Visualize your life as you wish it to be. Napoleon Bonaparte said, "Imagination rules the world." Imagination is one of the most powerful gifts we possess as humans.

- Start with being at peace with who you are. Practice peace, love, and benevolence in all areas of your life. Accept yourself just as you are, but always allow for improvement. Draw this awareness deep into your being by focusing on it during your visualization, meditation, and/or yoga sessions.

- Learn meditation. Consider seeking for a local meditation group, many of which offer free instruction and support. Do a little research and discover a meditation style that appeals to you and fulfills your needs. The styles vary widely to accommodate people's specific needs and desires.

- Control your attention. Consistently place your attention in the present moment as meditation and yoga encourages us to do. Bring yourself back to the now, over and over again, with deliberate intention. Take advantage of Dimension Two: Working/Functional Consciousness by being fully present in the moment with whatever you are doing.

- Discover or reintroduce yourself to yoga. Find a local studio or check out some online resources and videos. Remember, a healthy body leads to a healthy mind, and yoga is a form of exercise. Regular exercise promotes optimal levels of performance, healing, energy, and relaxation.

Resources

Brain Sync: www.brainsync.com. Learn more about brainwave technology plus gain access to sound wave technology and guided meditations.

iAwake Technologies: www.iawaketechnologies.com. Access brainwave and biofield entrainment with sophisticated technologies and consciousness enhancing tools.

Explore my website: www.awakenmypotential.com. Also, read my short best-selling book, *The Mindfulness Approach,* to learn about breathing, yoga, and meditation techniques.

Dr. Andrew Weil, M.D: www.drweil.com. Search "breathing" for specific breathing techniques.

Project-Meditation: www.project-meditation.org. Learn about meditation and examine information about different techniques.

Mindvalley: www.mindvalley.com. Founder Vishen Lakhiani has many excellent programs involving visualization, meditation, and yoga.

Yoga Journal: www.yogajournal.com. Discover more about yoga and meditation through the site's many articles, instruction, and videos.

Reminder: You can find all live resource links on the author's website at AwakenMyPotential.com.

Chapter Seventeen

Transformation

Simple Steps for a Life Makeover

An enjoyable aspect of life is that we can transform it at will. Even though our brains may be more pliable in our younger years, maturity can offer alternative perspectives and motivation to change. At any age, our brains are fully capable of increasing mass and adaptability.

Developing new neural connections is particularly advantageous to middle-aged and older individuals. As we age, it's common for people to lose neural plasticity, which is the ability of the brain to adapt to new information. This is probably where the phrase "you can't teach an old dog new tricks" originated.

Being open-minded and learning new things is paramount for synaptic growth and development.

Synapses are the points of contact at which information is transmitted between neurons. Having synapses enables us to form thoughts and remember things.

As we mature, these synapses can stagnate or diminish if not exercised and reinforced. Developing new ways of perceiving things; adopting new attitudes about situations, beliefs, and events; and instilling new behaviors can improve synaptic functions. Learning new hobbies or skills can be quite beneficial and may reduce the possibility of neurodegeneration.

Synaptogenesis is the formation of new synapses while neurogenesis is the birth of new neurons or brain cells. Our brains have the propensity to regenerate these neural connections and neurons. It is possible to transform our brains into more efficient and better-performing instruments to reshape how we think, remember, and behave.

According to a 2017 article in *Psychology Today* , a study was published in the journal *eLife* entitled "Adult-Born Neurons Modify Excitatory Synaptic

Transmission to Existing Neurons." Neuroscientists at the University of Alabama at Birmingham conducted a technologically-advanced study using mice to learn about the aging cycle of neurons and its effect on neural connections. They found that the combination of neurogenesis and neuroplasticity caused less-fit, older neurons to die off as lively, newborn neurons assumed control of existing neural circuits by creating more robust synaptic connections.

This natural process of "neural pruning" snips out any neurons that are not actively wired together into a network. The indication here for the purposes of realizing our full potential is to replace as many old neurons/neural connections as possible to give rise to fresh, new neurons/neural connections. It's this ability of the human body that was my saving from a particularly traumatic event in my life.

Many years ago, I was involved in a terrible automobile accident. The vehicle I was driving was hit from behind by two cars as I was turning off the highway. The driver of one car became distracted and hit the car behind me, careening that vehicle into the rear corner of my car while I was making a right turn.

My vehicle rolled several times and took out the entry gate to the business I was entering. The jolt from the initial hit from behind broke my seat from its hinges, causing severe whiplash with a brain contusion along with ruptured discs in my neck and spine.

The first few years of recovery were the most challenging. The burdensome ordeal caused me more grief than expected. It took considerable effort for me to concentrate and focus on my job and family. I was diagnosed with Post-traumatic stress disorder (PTSD) and Post-concussive syndrome (PCS).

I suffered from migraines, intense pain in my neck, distorted vision, and balance issues. I frequently became confused, disoriented, and depressed. This is not a good recipe for success in a high stress, upper management job working sixty to seventy hours per week.

It was particularly problematic with my teaching of martial arts. Before the accident, I was at the height of my physical conditioning, and I was preparing for my fourth degree master black belt in Tae Kwon Do, Chung Do Kwan where the mind/body connection is crucial to performance.

I was fortunate to test for my black belt master's degree with the late Grand Master Edward B. Sell and his wife, Grand Master Brenda Sell. It was not my best performance, and the testing was far more difficult than it should have been due to symptoms from the auto accident. However, with the deepest intentions and die-hard resolution, I was able to secure the fourth gold stripe on my black belt.

My unwavering desire for self-mastery and improvement is what got me through those tough times. I immersed myself in research, discovering means of adapting to the conditions at hand while inching my way toward healing.

My meditation practice yielded tremendous value as I struggled to regain my equanimity. It was, and still is, a long, arduous process of recovery that has reshaped me as a person. I am thrilled I was able to rebuild and restructure my damaged brain. You are never too old to rebuild and recover!

Dr. Daniel G. Amen is one of America's leading psychiatrists and brain health experts. He is a clinical neuroscientist and a ten-time New York Times best-selling author. He manages the world's largest database of functional brain scans relating to behavior, totaling over 140,000 scans on patients from 120 countries. In his book, *Change Your Brain, Change Your Life*, he shares means of improving cognitive functions such as memory, attention, emotional issues, and behavior.

Using SPECT scans (single-photon emission computed tomography), his team can analyze the blood flow and activity inside a person's brain. These scans display images of diminished brain tissue due to injury, stress, drug abuse, sleep deprivation, poor diet, lack of exercise, and other related issues. Once a problem is identified, his team can customize a treatment plan for healing.

Dr. Amen believes and has presented evidence that the brain can recover and rebuild itself by replacing neurons and synapses while regenerating new brain tissue. He has formulated a wide array of specific nutritional products to aid this regeneration and for optimizing and balancing brain function, energy, memory and learning, mood, stress reduction, and sleep.

In his book, Dr. Amen states:

> After looking at tens of thousands of brain scans, we began to think about the concept of "brain reserve." Brain reserve is the cushion of healthy brain tissue we have so we can deal with the unexpected stresses that come our way. The more reserve we have, the more resilient we are in times of trouble. The less reserve, the more vulnerable we are. Anything you do that harms your brain decreases its reserve.

Let me provide some examples to illustrate further:

- Chronic stress kills cells in the memory centers of the brain (the hippocampus).
- Brain injuries, concussions, or other types of head trauma cause physical damage.
- Poor diet and nutrition, too much alcohol or drug use (abuse), and environmental toxins compromise brain health.
- Constant negative thinking disrupts healthy brain function.
- Anything that decreases blood flow to the brain steals from your reserve, such as a lack of sleep, untreated sleep apnea, smoking, or too much caffeine.

You can increase your brain's reserve with a brain-healthy lifestyle. Your ability to change how you handle life's inevitable stressors can heal and transform your brain. When you change your brain, you transform your life.

Brain transformation occurs when we learn to adapt to and improve our attitudes, social skills, relationships, and physical and mental abilities. We can learn "new tricks" anytime in life. Once we obtain a better understanding of how our brains work, we are more able to advance proficiently in the direction of our desires. (Refer back to chapters fourteen and fifteen concerning how our brains work.)

While bettering our brains, and thus our lives, is certainly the goal, it isn't a "one and done" proposition. It's a lifetime learning and application. It can't be accomplished in a single exercise or positive thought.

I liken this to learning a game. If you wish to learn the game of chess, for example, you must develop an understanding of the game first. You need to think through what are the game pieces, what do they represent, and how are they moved. Then you progress to exploring what are the strategies, what are the possibilities, what are the rules, and how do you win.

Each step of learning this game must be performed in some succession. You cannot learn chess in one moment. It takes many moments, one after the other. But when that comes to a lifetime of learning and changing the landscape of your brain, isn't it an exciting realization?

There are no limits. New neural connections will support you during your weak times so you won't be so tempted to give up or give in. Remember, you can change *now* to improve your future.

Solutions

• Develop new neural connections and networks by learning new things. Whatever age you are, begin by expanding your awareness. Discover what interests you most and research it. Find a hobby or trade, join a club, write a book, participate in a fitness program, or read about parenting, social, or business skills.

• Build brain reserve by improving sleeping habits. If you can't get eight hours of sleep, get six hours of good sleep. Avoid smartphones, computer screens, and TV's at least one or two hours before bedtime. The light interferes with your sleep cycles.

- Go easy on yourself and de-stress as often as you can. Release guilt, forgive others, avoid being overwhelmed, and recover from stressful situations immediately by placing your complete attention in the present moment.

- Meditate, meditate, meditate! It will change your life. Don't wait for that perfect moment to begin your meditation routine. You can discover perfection in moments experienced during meditation.

- Overall, there is always more right with you than there is wrong with you. Refurbish the wrong and enhance the right.

- Play games with your mind. Research websites and apps that offer games to improve brain function.

Resources

Dr. Daniel Amen's Brain Health Assessment: www.brainhealthassessment.com. Take the free quiz available here.

Mindbodygreen: www.mindbodygreen.com. Search for the article "11 Powerful Questions That Can Help You Transform Your Life."

Psychology Today: www.psychologytoday.com. Search for the article "6 Steps to Transform Your Outlook.

Lumosity: www.lumosity.com. You can play more than sixty cognitive games.

Elevate: www.elevateapp.com. You can learn more than thirty-five personalized mind games to build communication and analytical skills.

BrainHQ: www.brainhq.com. Here you can learn to exercise your memory, attention, brain speed, people skills, and intelligence.

Reminder: You can find all live resource links on the author's website at AwakenMyPotential.com.

Chapter Eighteen

Transformoments

Moment By Moment Transformation

Life is a series of what I refer to as transformoments. In each moment we live, we have an opportunity to transform that moment into an enhanced sense of being. We can shift from lazy into active, from sadness into happiness, from uneducated into educated.

Look to revolutionize your life with transformational moments. Opportunities abound! Transformation can be easy or difficult, depending on your outlook. It's best to apply a positive, expectant mindset. When learning something new, for example, embrace the attitude "this is going to make me, not break me."

Begin by starting small. It's easier to create small transformations, one moment at a time, than it is to transform your entire life at once. You will most likely be enormously overwhelmed if you attempt to transform your whole life instantly. I have found that only those who have had an extremely profound experience or awakening, such as a near-death experience, are able to change their entire life in one step.

But small steps can have a big impact. The outcome of an entire three-hour football game can be transformed by one play in one moment. One player's shift in awareness, attitude, or energy level can drastically alter the game for either team.

Consider a defensive cornerback who is covering an offensive wide receiver going for a deep pass down field. He intentionally reaches through the outstretched arms of the receiver and meticulously snatches the ball before the receiver can wrap his hands around it. This cornerback is "in the zone."

Time slows down for him as his focus and conscious awareness peaks. He loses all sense of the crowd and the other players on the field. His attention becomes wholly absorbed in the intense play unfolding.

In an instant, the energy and excitement on the field and in the stands transitions from one team to the other. His transformoment leads to a game-changing victory for the defense.

Think of a time in your life when you purposefully changed your mind at the very last moment while on a project and it created brilliant success. How about a time during a conversation when you chose to be kind rather than being right and you made the other person feel delighted and valued? Moments like this are transformational because they change our lives, and potentially the lives of others, taking us up a level of being better.

Transformoments invite us to continue on the route to positive transformation. Each small gain we make builds upon another and then another.

Since you are reading this book, you are probably a lot like me in that you are looking for ways to improve your quality of life. For me, there is always room for improvement. I am continually seeking to reform many areas of my life. I will admit that the changes do not always come easy for me; I have to work at it and practice daily, or shall I say, moment by moment.

I am particularly pleased when evidence of successful tranformoments emerge. Growing, evolving, changing —it's all good! In my successes, I find gratitude, appreciation, and a sense of wellbeing. But I turn my failures into good as well. I find motivation, inspiration, forgiveness, and acceptance. Overall, the process intrigues me and inspires me to continue despite any missteps along the way.

When I was in sixth grade, an ESE (Exceptional Student Education) teacher pulled me out of my classroom. She told me I was far behind the other students in my reading skills. This was a total embarrassment for a twelve-year-old kid. Being taken from class in front of my peers mortified me to no end. I felt stupid and ashamed sitting in front of a reading monitor with the only other "learning disabled" student in the school. I spoke of this to no one.

Fortunately, I was so humiliated that it inspired me to excel in reading. I decided to make the most of it and remove myself from that environment as quickly as possible. My goal was using the moment to power my transformation. It was satisfying as I made great strides and was able to go back to my regular classroom full-time with my friends and fellow students within a few months.

Transformations can occur at any time in life. For some, they will manifest quickly and, perhaps, immediately. A person's life can transform in an instant with the birth of a child, a change in employment, a decision to avoid substance abuse, or a spiritual awakening.

For many of us, it can take months, years, or a lifetime to effect change. I look at transformation as an ongoing process, one step at a time. Each little win contributes to a sense of satisfaction and achievement.

Every time I encounter a positive shift, make a favorable decision, or decide to do the right thing, it creates an intention to improve myself in some way. I have been able to consciously create incredible, sacred moments of profound peace and clarity by taking advantage of my transformoments. Ideas, inspirations, answers to issues, all come to life and provide a deep sense of oneness and knowing. The doors open to awaken my potential and live the life I choose.

It can be the same for you too.

Solutions

- Place your complete attention in the present moment. Include transformoments in your everyday experience. Transform yourself one moment at a time. Give yourself permission to expand and develop into the person you wish to be. One small step can transition into one giant leap.

- You do not have to adopt my "unwavering desire for self-improvement." All it takes is a moderate desire to improve upon your situation. If you want a better life, get it! Just pick one thing and work on it. Once you have reached the goal and experienced its benefits to your satisfaction, work on another area of your life.

- Ask yourself the right questions. What interests me most in life? What can I do to improve my situation? How can I serve? What are my talents? Who can help me achieve my goals? These questions open the door to transforming yourself.

- Be positive! Eliminate as many negative thoughts as possible. Negative thinking reinforces tendencies toward illness, unhappiness, and stress. Make yourself aware each time negative thoughts enter your mind. Then, transition them into thoughts of affirmative acceptance, confidence, affirmation of intentions, forgiveness, gratitude, and peace. Focus on what you accomplished rather than on what you failed to accomplish. Fail forward; there is no real failure, only feedback. Realize that you are perfectly imperfect just the way you are.

Resources

Mindbodygreen: www.mindbodygreen.com. Search for the article "11 Powerful Questions That Can Help You Transform Your Life."

Psychology Today: www.psychologytoday.com. Search for the article "6 Steps to Transform Your Outlook."

Huffpost: www.huffpost.com. Search for the article "7 Steps to Transform Your Life."

Wall Street Insanity: www.wallstreetsanity.com. Search for the article "6 Ways to Transform Your Life in Less Than One Year."

Reminder: You can find all live resource links on the author's website at AwakenMyPotential.com.

Chapter Nineteen

Experience the Shift

Transcending From Average To Exceptional

Learning to move from consciousness into super-consciousness, where the unlimited mind and unrestricted potential resides, will significantly improve your outlook on life and the means by which you navigate your way.

Transcending the threshold into higher states of consciousness is a learned behavior. Those who are ready for change, ready to discover their true nature, ready to improve life skills, and ready to make a difference in the lives of those around them will leverage this knowledge and adapt more readily to events and circumstances in our ever-changing world.

The ability to immediately shift from negative emotional states into lighter, freer attitudes can be accomplished with knowledge and practice. In the preceding chapters, I have established many beneficial ways of elevating consciousness and altering lifestyles. Let us now go deeper.

A feeling of what you are is always stronger than a feeling of what you wish to be. In other words, feeling in the present as if you were already living your dreams is more powerful than just wanting it. Wishing upon something is merely a thought. Feeling something embodies it. It becomes a part of your nature, your expression. When thoughts translate into feelings, an expression of a new reality may occur.

To create your dream, you must feel what it feels like to own it, to live it, to be it. The more attention we place on something, the more real it becomes. The more feelings we ascribe to it, the more significant interactions we will experience between the brain, viscera, and the mind. This interaction completes the circuit within the entire body for optimal assimilation.

When we experience a visceral reaction, that deep body or gut reaction to a stimulus or experience, neurotransmitters (chemical messengers) are released that determine what emotions we feel and force a physical response of some sort.

For example, if you experience a driver dangerously cutting you off while on the highway, you may instantly feel anger, fear, or frustration. If your supervisor insults you or your performance in front of your peers, you may feel embarrassment, resentment, or humiliation.

Even though you can control these feelings based on your interpretation of the event and the choice you make to change your feelings, you will probably experience an immediate negative reaction and feel unwanted emotions.

Conversely, if you deliberately place yourself in a position to experience positive feelings, such as achieving a specific goal, then you can more easily control the outcome. You can experience the feelings that you want. You can feel how you want to feel instead of feeling restrained by the situation.

Let's say you want to experience profound relaxation. The first thing that happens is your thought of wanting to be relaxed. Next, you visualize in your mind laying on a lounge chair on a secluded beach with soaring birds and gentle ocean waves rolling rhythmically onto the shore. Within your mind, you hear the sounds of the birds' songs and the ocean waves breaking onto the sand. You see the beauty that presents itself, you smell the salt in the air, and you feel the warm, comforting breeze caressing your body.

Now, you are in a position to feel some emotions associated with such a scene, like peace, security, love, and appreciation. Your body has responded from the initial thought and then proceeded forward to the viscerally derived emotional responses resulting from your visualization.

This is applicable to any goal or intention that you seek. Think about what you want. Visualize it vividly in your mind using all of your senses, then enjoy the emotional responses this creates. Maintain your focus on these feelings and your desired outcome. If a negative thought or emotion slips in, return your attention to your visualization and the positive feelings evoked.

Mentally rehearse your intentions. This is a surefire way of garnering a sense of satisfaction that you are moving toward your intention. Goals and intentions establish excitement and enthusiasm in your life. It sets the course for achievement and satisfaction. Even though you may not achieve your specific goal, you will have a stronger opportunity for success if you mentally rehearse what you want to achieve.

The fact that you experienced achievement within your mind accelerates real-world potential. Our universe is based on potentials. Your mind cannot determine the difference between what is vividly imagined and actual reality. After all, reality may only exist within the mind.

If you create the reality within your mind that you truly desire, you may very well alter your waking reality. We do not yet fully understand the quantum world, but this is where unlimited potential resides, and we may be more capable than we think of transforming our lives based on these potentials.

Do beliefs precede experience?

There is a great deal of discussion of whether experience precedes belief or belief precedes experience. If you believe that your experiences determine what beliefs you hold as truth, then your life will reflect experiences that create your beliefs, and you will be guided or controlled by those beliefs. You will, in effect, be living your life according to the uncontrollable circumstances that are placed in your path.

If you believe that your beliefs precede your experiences, as I do, then you will be more in control of your experiences based on the beliefs you *choose* to hold. Your life then revolves around *you,* making the choices to believe as you will.

In 1986, Folgers Coffee introduced a television commercial featuring the famous Tavern on the Green restaurant in New York City. Evidently, they substituted Folgers Coffee for the restaurant's fine coffee and used hidden cameras to reveal the results.

When customers were told they had actually been served Folgers instead, they were amazed and hardly believed it was Folgers Coffee, but they loved it! Their beliefs preceded their experience. Because they believed they were to be served the famous restaurant's gourmet coffee, their experience reflected the results they expected.

It's a matter of perspective that translates into reality. Beliefs encapsulate feelings. A thought is essentially a physical thing that enters or is produced in your mind. When we transmute a thought into a feeling, it affects our mind and our body. A thought can be powerful. A feeling can be even more powerful.

Feelings are experienced viscerally. This is where the heart of intuition lies. We intuit events and situations viscerally which then produces impulses that can guide us to make the correct decisions. When our intuition is engaged, we are crossing the threshold into higher consciousness.

It is in our gut that we feel and intuit. There are about 200 million neurons in the enteric nervous system that governs the function of the gastrointestinal tract. It is actually our second brain. The enteric nervous system operates in a similar fashion to the brain in our heads. It creates the "gut feeling" that guides us to make intuitive decisions. The brain and the gut work in synchronicity with mind to create our experience of life.

Think of all the systems within your body working synchronistically to perform their basic operations. You have the respiratory; digestive; endocrine; cardiovascular; nervous systems including sympathetic, parasympathetic, enteric and central nervous system; musculoskeletal; renal/urinary; lymphatic/immune, and reproductive systems—all of which are vital for the survival of our species.

Continue this line of thinking. Consider how the vast, complex systems of our earth, which include wildlife, plant life, minerals, soil, air, and water, all work in accord for the continuance of life. The entire universe seems to operate within this fashion.

Mind is the body. Mind is the planet. Mind is the universe. It is mind, this universal intelligence that pervades all things. This field of mind interconnects all of life in ways we do not yet completely understand. It may not be personality-based intelligence.

Personality is a construct of the brain relating to one's beliefs, emotions, and tendency of action. The universal mind, however, seems to be information-based. It appears that we experience this data exchange without consciously being aware of it much of the time.

Either this system was set into motion at some point or it has always been. Regardless of that, our entire existence depends on how we interact with this information exchange. When we ignore this exchange or disrespect it, we suffer. When we abuse or neglect each other, when we denude our forests or pollute our oceans, when we disregard our own body's health, we suffer the consequences.

When we are in alignment with each other and our environment and allow ourselves to exchange information with the field (universal mind), all things come together in coherence. This symbiotic relationship is the foundation of life itself.

Solutions

- Be in the present moment. Learn to feel your way through life. Feelings are more powerful than thoughts.

- Force physical responses based on the feelings you wish to experience. Use your imagination and visualization involving all of your senses to fully bring your desired feelings to life.

- Replay events in your mind, vividly, the way you want to experience them and not how you would normally react. Respond instead of react.

- Repeatedly practice changing states. Move from low energy to high energy, transition from over-thinking to relaxed and open, change from a negative perspective to a positive mindset. The more you practice, the easier it will be to gain control of your emotions.

- Beliefs precede experience. Discover your unrevealed hindering beliefs and transform them into empowering beliefs.

Resources

Positive Psychology Program: www.positivepsychologyprogram.com. Search for the article "How to Live in the Present Moment: 35 Exercises and Tools (+ Quotes)."

Psychology Today: www.psychologytoday.com. Search for the article "The Psychology and Philosophy of Imagination."

Forbes: www.forbes.com. Search for the article "Emotions Have Energy: What Energy Are You Sending?"

Reminder: You can find all live resource links on the author's website at AwakenMyPotential.com.

Chapter Twenty

Luminance

Activate Your Higher Self

Luminance can be described as being bathed in light. A state of luminance is one of enlightenment. The Buddhists refer to this as being without desire or the need to suffer. Your life does not have to be perfect or even close to perfect to attain some level of luminance.

Every day, common man enlightenment can be achieved in small or large doses by anyone. You don't have to be a Buddhist Monk or an Indian Yogi guru to attain some form of luminance. It is just a state of being that:

- Allows us to be at peace with who we are.
- Helps us to see and understand that we are intrinsic to the whole of humanity.

- Helps us navigate our way through life with a sense of knowing and allowance in the field of universal mind.

Moments of illumination are created in my meditation practice. Countless times I have received the answers to difficult problems during or shortly after meditation. Ideas and inspirations have surfaced as a result of my meditation sessions. However, these things can happen anytime and any place.

From a position of luminance, we can live from the perspective of "how can I contribute and how may I serve?" We should not wait until the perfect opportunity to serve. Every day presents many opportunities to contribute and aid others.

At some point in our personal development, we should no longer be content to believe in truths established by others, but rather seek in our innermost self those truths that satisfy the evolution of humanity rather than the ego.

Your innermost self, or higher self, realizes that you are enough just as you are. Your ego mind may have a desire to prove to others that you are more than you appear to be. Your ego may want to feel important, needed, or wanted. Your highest nature is not dependent on what others may think of you.

Consider the person who wants to become the CEO of a major company in order to validate his or her self, driven by the ego for narcissistic or monetary values. This self-serving mindset can lead to a sense of incompleteness. How many famous, successful entrepreneurs, actors, or entertainers commit suicide or overdose with drugs due to their being unhappy with life? They may be worth millions or billions of dollars and still cannot achieve true success with the lives they are leading.

Success cannot be measured in dollars, but instead with the realization of inner peace and harmony, of luminance and enlightenment. Those who seek happiness in power or fortune frequently miss out on the true meaning of life. To fulfill the soul is to coexist within the field of mind, with the two working together, synchronistically for the good of all.

Solutions

- Quiet your brain chatter with meditation, music, breathing, or whatever means that work for you so your intuition can come to fruition. It is hard to achieve a higher plane of being when your brain is overloaded.

- Break away from the ego mind and transition into universal mind in order to see yourself as a part of a larger continuum.

- Adopt the approach of serving others with an attitude of interconnectedness. Even the smallest gestures, such as sharing a smile, can show a serving heart.

- Ask questions of how and what rather than why. Examples are "How can I improve my situation? What can I do to make immediate changes?" These questions encourage us to search the universal mind for illumined answers.

Resources

Web MD: www.webmd.com. Search for the article "How to Quiet Your Mind."

Huffpost: www.huffingtonpost.com. Search for the article "How to Drop Your Ego With 5 Techniques."

Steve Pavlina: www.stevepavlina.com. Search for the article "Do Your Beliefs Reflect Reality or Create It?"

Reminder: You can find all live resource links on the author's website at AwakenMyPotential.com.

Chapter Twenty-One

Creating Your Reality

Manifest Your Dreams

How do we go about creating the life we desire? That is an easy question to ask, but a complex one to answer. There are many factors involved in the creation process.

Much of it depends on our outlook on life and our current situation. Also, our past events and experiences have a tremendous influence on us. In some countries, people are politically oppressed or deprived of their rights. Many exist in extreme poverty and violence, and it may be virtually impossible for them to improve the quality of life in ways they desire.

Regardless of severe circumstances, people do rise above abject conditions to live peaceful, loving, and meaningful lives. It may be complicated and challenging, but it is certainly achievable.

For those of us who live manageable, uncomplicated lives, the journey can be simpler and more straightforward. It stands to reason that those whose lives are replete with all the resources necessary to live comfortably without fear of oppression, failure, or poverty should have a smoother transition into creating a satisfying reality.

Having said that, even those who are fortunate can have a difficult time effecting positive changes due to job situations, ill health, relationship issues, or a host of other stressful circumstances. Childhood events, personality traits, past trauma, and religious beliefs can interfere with designing the ideal life.

Whatever your circumstances, make the decision to strive for improvement. Be willing to step beyond your comfort level and utilize some of the techniques we have explored in this book.

My wife and I have a number of large oak trees in our one-acre yard. Late in Florida's winter, the leaves begin to fall over several weeks. With an afternoon breeze, thousands of leaves will detach themselves from their branches and rain down, glistening in the bright sunshine and adorning the lawn with a veil of beauty. Then, as spring approaches, a wonder of fresh, brilliant green foliage emerges to grace us with its majestic beauty.

It reminds me of how we have to lose all of the old habits, beliefs, and the ego before we can sprout forth our newly created selves.

When we create something, we cause it to come into being, as something unique, that would not naturally evolve. We construct from our thoughts or imagination, as a work of art, an invention, or a way of being.

Some things can take an enormous amount of time to create, such as a building a successful business or a skyscraper, learning to dance, or acquiring a new language. Other things can be created quickly, like changing an emotional state, managing attention, adopting a new belief, doing or saying something nice, initiating a goal, or meditating.

A series of small steps can rapidly develop into substantial gains. A multitude of minor tweaks can immensely alter a golfer's game. Beginning with short, easy steps and then progressing into more difficult routines is the ideal. Better your game one move at a time.

Create what you want, but do not create on top of similar issues. You can create a change for the moment, but you must go back and fix whatever correlated problems you have at some point. It's like a computer with a pop-up warning; you can click the notification off repeatedly but it will keep popping back up until you resolve the issue.

In other words, if you decide you are going to be more outgoing and sociable at parties or meetings but you hold a belief that you are introverted, then you will need to undo this belief because it will undoubtedly interfere with accomplishing your goal. Initiate your goal and then work on the conflicting belief as well.

To demonstrate the simplicity of creating within, let's take a minute to perform an easy exercise. Within your mind, create a feeling of happiness. Even if you are not happy with your life's circumstances at the moment, feel what it would feel like to be happy. Remember a time when you won an award, witnessed the birth of your child, received a desired gift, fell in love, vacationed in a beautiful place, enjoyed a fantastic meal, spent time with a best friend, got a promotion…you get the idea.

Are you able to get in touch with those feelings of happiness? Even if it was just a fleeting moment, did you feel happiness?

The trick now is to recognize the feeling of happiness so you can repeat it and apply it to more stressing situations again and again. Knowing and doing this will allow you to create the feeling of being happy at will. Once the unpleasant or stressful event has passed (or even during it), you can immediately create happy feelings. Just place your attention on past events that evoked those feelings.

Even if you feel only an ephemeral moment of happiness, it will clear up space in your brain to view your situation in a different light. Once this process is repeated again and again, new neural pathways will begin to evolve, and it will become easier to change states at will.

I keep pictures of my family, friends, positive quotes, and my pet on my office desk and wall. Just looking at them in times of stress calms me down, clears the brain clutter, and makes me happy.

Most important in creating a happier emotional state is practicing what I call the 4R's—Realize, Recover, Realign, and Refocus. First, we must heighten our awareness in times of stress and *Realize* our present emotional state. Then, we can begin to *Recover* by re-framing our situation. Then, we *Realign* with our intentions. Finally, we *Refocus* on the present moment and harness the power of the field of mind.

Remember, the only thing between you and your issue is your thoughts and beliefs about it. The event has no inherent meaning. Merely shift your thoughts to bring about change.

If you learn to ask the right questions of yourself when you are seeking to *Realize*, then your answers will be more engaging and suitable for your current situation.

For instance, asking "why" when exploring the tough event usually elicits negative responses based on past experiences and beliefs. Let's pretend you ask yourself, "Why am I always afraid to speak my mind when I am with others?" Watch as the self-deflating beliefs then pop instantly into your mind—because I am incompetent, because I am shy, because other people won't get me, because I may say the wrong thing, because I may embarrass myself.

Maybe these negative thoughts formed when you were young and in school during a time you expressed your opinion and were ridiculed by your classmates and perhaps even your teacher. Now, when you attempt to express your thoughts in the company of others, those old feelings of embarrassment rise to the surface and stifle you.

They are certainly the enemy of creating a happier state as needed in the present moment. At this point, you will want to eliminate those old beliefs. (Read, or reread, chapters six, seven, and eleven for help with eliminating misperceived beliefs.)

By learning to ask "how" or "what" questions, you can empower yourself and *Recover*. Ask yourself, "What can I do to change this behavior? What can I learn that will help me speak openly without fear of embarrassment? What can I do to improve my speaking skills? What can I do to eliminate the hesitation of speaking my mind?"

"How" and "what" questions challenge the mind to seek answers that will fulfill the need of positive change in place of digressing it into past, undesirable memories.

Let's explore another example that illustrates how you can *Realign*. Pause and create a sacred moment. If you are a religious person who believes in God as the supreme being, then feel what it would feel like to be one with your God. Embrace the love and feel that warm, loving essence flowing through you. Allow your mind and body to be imbued with a divine sense of oneness and belonging.

If you are not a religious person, then feel the energy of universal mind, of unlimited potential. Feel the oneness of all creation. Experience the wonder of nature and the connection we share with all that is. Feel the interwoven thread of life that permeates all of humanity.

Make it your paradise, your private sanctum where you can feel safe and at peace. Visualize yourself in a church, cathedral, temple, forest, mountaintop, ocean, or a distant star or planet where peace and love exist in harmony with all. Feel what it would feel like to be in this place where there is no stress, no suffering, no desires. You are content, happy, and reside in the joyous expression of who you are as a being of light and love.

Use your imagination to create the scene, replete with surroundings of beautiful, docile birds and animals, lush forests, intricate architecture, ornate altars and pillars, meandering streams, or extraordinary vistas. Fully engage all of your senses. Generate the sights, sounds, smells, tastes, and feelings as if you were there in the flesh.

Once you have created within your mind and fully experienced this sacred place, you will probably notice that your heart rate has decreased to a steady, healthy pace. Your breathing has also slowed, your mind has become quiet, and your body is still.

This is a place you can return to anytime you wish. This sacred place allows you to recharge and replenish your energy. It will enable you to expand beyond your everyday experience of life into a more fulfilling sense of the real you, the one who is infinite intelligence, unlimited potential, and the very expression of life itself.

You can also create a disposition of non-reaction. This is where you learn not to label events as you perceive them. If you find yourself continually reacting negatively to the behaviors of others, you can condition yourself to avoid the reaction.

Each time you find yourself reacting negatively to a situation, envelop yourself in the awareness of that feeling. Acknowledge the feeling, don't resist it, and decide not to react. Make a conscious effort to experience non-reactive emotion. Then switch to employing the 4R's.

Let's say that your supervisor belittles you in the presence of your peers and, instantly, you react with anger. Realize the feelings that have arisen, recover from them by placing your attention on creating no reaction, and then realign yourself with your intention of allowing the comments to be as they are, which is words. They have no impact on you unless you give them power.

Remember, this is merely an event and events have no meaning. The feelings that result from an event are those of which you have created. When you learn to create non-reaction, you control your environment.

Stress is reduced and a feeling of satisfaction and empowerment ensues.

Solutions

- Be in the present moment. Learn to feel your way through life. Feelings are more powerful than thoughts.

- Force your physical responses based on the feelings you wish to experience. Use your imagination and visualization skills by involving all of your senses. Replay events in your mind, vividly, the way you want to experience them and not how you would normally react. Respond instead of react.

- Repeatedly practice changing states. The more you practice, the easier it will be to gain control of your emotions.

- Beliefs precede experience, a topic explored in chapter nineteen. Discover your unrevealed hindering beliefs and transform them into empowering beliefs.

- Breakaway from the ego mind and transition into universal mind. Your dreams will manifest more easily when you adopt the approach of serving others with an attitude of interconnectedness.

- Ask questions of "how" and "what" rather than "why." Examples are "How can I improve my situation? What can I do to make immediate changes?"

- Use the 4R's. 1. *Realize* your problem and identify with it. 2. *Recover* from it by identifying what could be worse than your problem. 3. *Realign* back into coherency by recognizing that you are better off than the alternative. 4. *Refocus* on your positive intentions and goals in the present moment.

Resources

Positive Psychology Program: www.positivepsychologyprogram.com. Search for the article "How to Live in the Present Moment: 35 Exercises and Tools (+ Quotes)."

Psychology Today: www.psychologytoday.com. Search for the article "The Psychology and Philosophy of Imagination."

Forbes: www.forbes.com. Search for the article "Emotions Have Energy: What Energy Are You Sending?"

Inc: www.inc.com. Search for the article "7 Questions You Should Ask Yourself Today to Become a Better Person Tomorrow."

IQ Matrix: www.blog.iqmatrix.com. Search for the article "How To Get What You Want Faster Through Asking Better Questions."

Web MD: www.webmd.com. Search for the article "How to Quiet Your Mind."

HuffPost: www.huffingtonpost.com. Search for the article "How to Drop Your Ego With 5 Techniques."

Steve Pavlina: www.stevepavlina.com. Search for the article "Do Your Beliefs Reflect Reality or Create It?"

Reminder: You can find all live resource links on the author's website at AwakenMyPotential.com.

Chapter Twenty-Two

Approaching The Threshold

The Crucial Steps of Your Awakening

The two aspects of reality are the known and the unknown. Our everyday, waking reality is in the known world. The unknown world is the infinite field of the mind within the realm of quantum entanglement. Most of us tend to operate within the physical domain of the known with little interaction in the unknown. We can attain a more balanced life when we move toward the unknown on a moment by moment basis.

With every opportunity we take to immerse ourselves in the unknown, our intuitive mind will allow us to move into higher states of being. This is where life becomes more meaningful, rewarding, appealing, and engaging. This transformation can occur at any stage in life. Whatever your state of self-incurred emotional distress, psychological brokenness, or physical debilitation, you have the freedom to adopt new avenues of your choice for personal advancement and development.

The Seven Cardinal Gates

The Seven Cardinal Gates is a means by which we can shift our awareness from the known into the unknown. This system came to me immediately following a morning meditation several years ago. It is a series of simple, yet highly effective, steps toward elevating levels of consciousness. It is a sequential approach to opening your mind to achieve the following states, ultimately resulting in a sense of wellbeing.

The Seven Gates are:
1. Thankfulness
2. Love
3. Appreciation
4. Forgiveness
5. Gratitude
6. Peace
7. Wellbeing

Psalms 100.4 of the Bible, King James Version, states, "Enter into his gates with thanksgiving, and into his courts with praise: be thankful unto him, and bless his name." (Whether this is in reference to your God or the field of mind, is yours to decipher.)

Thankfulness. We begin the journey by entering the gates with thanksgiving. We access the divine field with a thankful heart. When we are thankful, the doors open to elevate our sense of oneness and lightheartedness. Once we are thankful, we can then more easily allow love to begin to flow in our lives.

Love. As we experience love, this gate swings wide open to welcome a sense of nurturing, companionship, connectedness, and selflessness. When we love, our spirits rise to encompass the whole of humanity. We are free from judgment, jealousy, and vindictiveness. We discover the good in others and ourselves, and we can more readily transition into appreciation.

Appreciation. When we appreciate, we can be fully conscious of the conditions that shape our lives and that of others. We respect the trials, transitions, behaviors, and difficulties as well as the triumphs of others and ourselves in a compassionate manner. When we are in the position to fully appreciate, then we are more able to transition into forgiveness.

Forgiveness. Experiencing forgiveness can be exceedingly liberating. It frees our minds and hearts to expand and mature into higher states of consciousness. It allows us to move beyond the limitations of the ego. It's the ultimate redeemer. In forgiveness, we are now more receptive to gratitude.

Gratitude. Being grateful silences desire. The want for personal gain is suppressed. When we are grateful for our lives, families, relationships, jobs, homes, and freedoms, it becomes easier for us to cope with the stresses of our daily routines. In gratitude, we can move directly into a feeling of peace.

Peace. When we are at peace with ourselves and others, we become expansive and open. The ego is diminished and the need for validation is squelched. Stressors become trivial rather than debilitating. A peaceful person is one who adapts effortlessly, without struggle, to the demands of life. When feeling peaceful, we can comfortably shift into wellbeing.

Wellbeing. In wellbeing, our concerns are not only about ourselves but others. We feel good about our state of mind and our status in life. We seek to improve the lives of others by offering assistance and support. We are less likely to succumb to the pressures of life. Wellbeing is characterized by good health, prosperity, love, and unity. Even if you are not physically or mentally well, you can experience wellbeing.

These seven steps represent a gradated approach to crossing the thresholds of elevated levels of consciousness.

When we find ourselves retreating into the ego, fight or flight stress, judgment, or any negative emotions, we can use these seven principal gates to bring us back into alignment.

This process of ascending into higher states of mind is easy to learn and can be completed in sixty seconds or so. With a little practice, one can achieve a state of wellbeing in a very short amount of time.

Each time you enter the gates, you will become more proficient. The more time you spend in any of these gates, the better your life will become. Navigating our lives in super consciousness is the ideal.

Typically, we are either approaching or retreating from higher levels of consciousness. It is generally not possible for most of us to remain static for extended periods. Einstein initially thought the universe was static, but, as discovered later, it is actually inflationary and constantly expanding, just as we want our consciousness to be.

There are a number of ways to integrate this process, and we will review each of them following a discussion and practice session of how to experience each of the gates effectively.

To begin, find a quiet place where you will not be disturbed. Sit comfortably and take three long, slow, deep breaths. Inhale to the count of seven and exhale to the same count. Relax your body and breathe slowly and effortlessly.

Calm the chatter in your brain by placing your complete attention on the feeling of thankfulness. Feel what it feels like to be thankful. Remember a time when you were particularly thankful for receiving a desired gift, pay raise, home-cooked meal, compliment, or another generous offering. Really get in touch with that feeling. Place your attention entirely on it and allow yourself to be consumed with thankfulness.

Experience all of the sensations and emotions associated with being thankful. Where do you feel it in your body? Recreate how you felt at the very moment you received it. Is it visceral? Do you feel it in your heart?

If you were able to connect with thankfulness and make it real to you effectively, then continuing through the Seven Gates will generate opportunities to move into deeper, more expansive states rapidly.

If you were not able to fully experience thankfulness, then I suggest practicing this short exercise several more times. In the learning stages, it is most beneficial to initiate this process in a quiet environment with a relaxed body and a still mind.

Remember, this is much more about feeling than thinking. First, you think of thankfulness and then immediately transition into the feeling and remain there until the next gate.

Repeat this same process with each of the other gates until you can experience all of them completely. You should feel relaxed, connected, and expansive. When you *become* thankfulness, love, appreciation, forgiveness, gratitude, peace, and wellbeing, your sense of oneness and wholeness will expand and evolve into a more positive view of your world.

Time appears to slow down, your brain becomes quiet, your heart begins to open, and your consciousness expands. This is where life develops more meaning and cohesiveness. It is an integrative approach to life itself.

Once you feel comfortable with the process, you can experiment with different ways of utilizing the gates to your benefit. There are seven progressive methods I employ to bring about transformation to my way of thinking, and thus, my life.

Method 1: The Feels

Begin by feeling what thankfulness feels like. Experience it fully. Then continue to feeling love, appreciation, forgiveness, gratitude, peace, and wellbeing. Take as much time as you need. The more you practice, the faster the results.

Method 2: The I Am's

Begin by stating, "I am thankfulness" and then feel it entirely. "I am love, I am appreciation, I am forgiveness, I am gratitude, I am peace, I am wellbeing." You may finish with the phrase "I am that, I am." Adding this phrase to the above statements solidifies your intentions. My perspective on this phrase is, "I am *that* particular thing, yes, I am."

Method 3: The Offerings

Begin by stating, "Thank you, for I am thankfulness." You are able to offer thanks to others because you are thankful. With this option, you envelop yourself with others and become intrinsic to the whole of humanity. You share the experience of thankfulness with everyone.

This exercise can also be performed with a certain person in mind. It may also be executed with yourself in mind. Speak the words to yourself as if you were talking to your inner child.

Continue with "I love you, for I am love; I appreciate you, for I am appreciation; I forgive you, for I am forgiveness; I am grateful for you, for I am gratitude; peace be with you, for I am peace; be well, for I am wellbeing."

Method 4: The Prayer

Begin by praying for another person stating "Thank you, I love you, I appreciate you, I forgive you, I am grateful for you, peace be with you, be well." This takes the focus off of you and directs it toward a specific individual, group, or even the world. It can deepen relationships with family, significant others, friends, or coworkers as it is a transformation into deeper care for them.

Method 5: The Meditation

Begin your meditation practice with the I Am's or any of the other options, like The Prayer. It's a great way to slow the mind and body down to enter into a meditative state. (Read chapter sixteen for more about meditation.)

Method 6: The Prep

Perform the I Am's in preparation for a meeting, speech, presentation, interview, family gathering, travel, or any situation that you would like to be more present, connected, and clear-minded. This process will quiet your mind and allow you to express yourself or perform in a more meaningful way.

Method 7: The Reciprocation

Begin with The Prayer option by addressing a specific individual and visualize their mirrored response. You say "Thank you" and imagine they say to you "Thank you." You say "I love you" and they return "I love you." You say "I appreciate you" and they respond "I appreciate you." Continue on: "I forgive you…I forgive you. I am grateful for you…I am grateful for you. Peace be with you…peace be with you. Be well…be well."

This option allows you the freedom to interact with another in ways you may not be able to in a person-to-person conversation (although, person-to-person interaction is ideal). You connect with this person in another dimension. This is particularly helpful in developing or healing relationships. It tends to assist you in viewing this person in a different light while opening your heart to their needs.

As you can see, The Seven Cardinal Gates is a powerful process that can change your life in a brief amount of time. With just a minimal amount of practice, significant gains can be realized. Within a few sessions on my own, I was able to complete the process in less than thirty seconds. Recently, I was shaken with the disturbing news of a friend's suicide. I used The Seven Gates to bring myself back into an emotionally stable state.

Shortly after I learned the Seven Gates, I recorded my voice speaking the seven gates and allowed about ten seconds in between. Even though it took a bit more time in some gates to get a good feel for it, I was able to speed the process up a little and stay on track. Recording the passage also solidified my intentions and allowed my brain to hear my spoken words which enabled my subconscious mind to accept it more readily.

Once you have practiced for a while, you should be able to feel each of the gates on a profound level instantly. Even if it takes you a few minutes, the reward can be immeasurable. You too can achieve fantastic results represented by each of The Seven Gates.

Remember to focus on the process and not the outcome. The results will bear the fruits of your practice. Once you have a handle on it, each time you say the words *thanks, thank you, I love you, I appreciate that/you, I forgive you/them, I am grateful, I am peace, peace be with you, I am well, be well,* or any use of the seven gates, you will immediately experience the feelings of those meanings in a way you have not felt before. They will be more real to you.

Anytime you are feeling doubt, fear, or any negative emotion or upset, take yourself through The Seven Gates. If you are angry, bitter, or resentful, complete the process fully to redirect yourself.

Solutions

• Practice The Seven Cardinal Gates until you feel comfortable enough to engage at will.

- Experiment with each of the seven options.

- In all things, focus on the process instead of the outcome.

Resources

Huffpost Life, The Blog: www.huffpost.com. Search for the article "How to Focus on the Process Instead of the Outcome."

CNBC Make it: www.cnbc.com. Search for the article "How Being Thankful Can Boost Your Well-Being and Success, According to Science."

Psychology Today: www.psychologytoday.com. Search for the article "Learning to Love and Be Loved."

Forbes: www.forbes.com. Search for the article "8 Ways To Have More Gratitude Every Day."

Power of Positivity: www.powerofpositivity.com. Search for the article "Psychologists Explain How To Forgive And Truly Let Go Of The Past."

Huffpost Life: www.huffpost.com. Search for the article "7 Ways to Experience Peace...Right Now!."

Reminder: You can find all live resource links on the author's website at AwakenMyPotential.com.

Chapter Twenty-Three

Compassionate Entrainment

Implementing Passion and Compassion

Many years ago, I attended a few life-changing seminars hosted by Avatar EPC that focused on managing belief systems, learning to operate in higher dimensions, and creating a desired lifestyle. Harry Palmer designed the material for the seminars.

The Avatar Compassion Exercise from the book *Resurfacing* by Harry Palmer is a beautiful lesson in appreciation. Let's take a more in-depth look at the third step of The Seven Gates—Appreciation—with the following activity that explores compassion.

Compassion Exercise: This exercise can be done anywhere that people congregate (airports, malls, parks, beaches, etc.). It should be done on strangers, unobtrusively, from some distance. Try to do all five steps on the same person.

Step 1
With attention on the person, repeat to yourself:
"Just like me, this person is seeking some happiness for his/her life."

Step 2

With attention on the person, repeat to yourself:
"Just like me, this person is trying to avoid suffering in his/her life."

Step 3

With attention on the person, repeat to yourself:
"Just like me, this person has known sadness, loneliness, and despair."

Step 4

With attention on the person, repeat to yourself:

"Just like me, this person is seeking to fulfill his/her needs."

Step 5

With attention on the person, repeat to yourself: "Just like me, this person is learning about life."

Be a walking beacon of the representation of The Seven Cardinal Gates. Emanate an outward expression of thankfulness, love, appreciation, forgiveness, gratitude, peace, and wellbeing.

Project them from your heart by imagining a field encapsulating your body and radiating out several feet and then gradually expanding further and further out offering love and blessings to all.

I've always been passionate about following the path less traveled, one who is perpetually curious about life, how it works and why it works the way it does. There is far more to life than just carving out a living, raising a family, and structuring time for fun and relaxation, although I enjoy all of these immensely.

I have always sought out the deeper meanings of spirituality, cognitive function, and the workings of the universe. My eternal curiosity has led me on a journey of self-exploration and self-improvement. Each day I find myself experimenting with new ways of defining and enhancing my reality.

I write books that are replete with information on how I am improving my life. My desire to change my behaviors and thinking patterns drive me to pursue alternative approaches. Life is not so easy for me due to my extreme expectations of life. I want more, and I expect more.

For a moment, think about driving one car for each area of your personal/family, business, and spiritual lives. You may be driving your personal/family car at 40mph, your business car at 70mph, and your spiritual car at 10mph. Over the course of one hour, you have traveled 40 miles in your personal/family car, 70 miles in your business car, and only 10 miles in your spiritual car.

How much ground do you anticipate covering within these areas of life? Are your driving habits consistent with your goals and intentions? If you wish to cover more terrain in your spiritual life, you may want to increase your speed in that car. By balancing your car's usage, you can achieve coherence and convert the image of your faith into reality.

The things you do today will either come back to help you or haunt you. The Threshold Approach is about becoming more conscious and skillful with your life.

Entrainment can occur when you follow the flow of another's experience. If a favorite coworker loses a family member to cancer, the other coworkers often feel the loss as well. We can quickly become entrained and synchronized with others' feelings.

The same is true for moments of happiness. A coworker or friend wins a battle against cancer, and everyone celebrates in harmony with them. Humans are easily entrained with the emotions of each other.

Deliberately look for opportunities to entrain others into positive states of being as often as you can. Bring others along with you on the path to joy, freedom, bliss, and expansion.

Solutions

• Become more compassionate by practicing the Compassion Exercise often.

• Entrain your thoughts and feelings with your higher self and with those around you who are positive in nature.

• Practice removing your focus on yourself and place it instead on others.

• Empathy is powerful. Use it to be more acceptant of others and their behaviors.

• Join an organization that focuses on helping others financially, spiritually, or otherwise.

Resources

Avatar: www.avatarepc.com. Discover new ways of navigating life with the articles and videos available on this site.

Greater Good Magazine: www.greatergood.berkeley.edu. Search for the article "Six Habits of Highly Compassionate People."

Zen Habits: www.zenhabits.net. Search for the article "A Guide to Cultivating Compassion in Your Life, With 7 Practices."

Reminder: You can find all live resource links on the author's website at AwakenMyPotential.com.

Chapter Twenty-Four

Handling Interference

The Tools For Smart Living

This last chapter is devoted to handling the day-to-day interruptions that interfere with your mental and emotional balance.

I know this last chapter is a bit longer than the others in this book, but if you stay with me, you'll learn several strategies for coping with daily living you can put in place immediately.

One of the greatest attributes we can possess in life is tenacity. It is the ability to keep getting back up on your feet every time you are knocked down by one of life's unpleasant surprises. When you get to the point where you can quickly rebound from adversity and not get swallowed up in the drama unfolding, then you will feel more like you are in the driver's seat.

273

Let's explore a number of tools and techniques that can be used to help you deal with moments of unbalance in your life.

Biofield Meditation

Data overload is certainly common in today's world. But did you know it can create blockages in energy movement and destabilize your biofield leaving dark, empty holes? This feeling of overwhelm feeds off your energy field, leaving it weak and unable to sustain its full effectiveness. The following visualization meditation will assist you in clearing away the clutter of unwanted stressors and negative emotions incurred by adverse experiences.

To practice the biofield meditation, find a quiet place where you will not be disturbed for ten minutes or so. Take a long, slow, deep breath in and hold it for three seconds, then exhale completely. Inhale slowly and deeply again, holding it for three seconds once more. Exhale completely, emptying your lungs and preparing them for another inhale. Inhale one last time, slowly and deeply. Hold it for three seconds and then exhale.

Relax your mind and body, releasing all tension while breathing normally.

Within your mind, visualize your perception of your existing energy field emanating from the visceral section of your body (just below your navel). Ideally, you should "see" it as spherical shape extending out from you about six feet in all directions. Notice the massive quantities of energy particles emanating from you within this bubble.

Observe its shape, colors, density, and feeling. Notice how it feels warm and safe inside the field. Feel deeper and deeper into this protective and healing vibrational energy held within this spherical field of light as it swirls and circulates in and around you.

Become one with your electromagnetic energy field. You, your body, and your biofield are all one and the same. Feel what it feels like to be the field. Feel the light, colors, density, warmth, and any sensations and fluctuations while sinking deeper into the subtleties of this field.

Examine the outer edges of your biofield and notice if there are any dark spots or holes. If there are, begin to swirl and circulate within your sphere, spreading energy and light into all areas, eliminating any dark spots or holes. If there are no dark areas, swirl within your sphere, circulating and intensifying the light and energy.

Now, acknowledge that your field is seamless, dense with energy, complete, and wholly encompassing as it begins to expand further and further out. Continue expanding the outer edges of your living energy field. It may extend out a few feet, a few miles, or a few galaxies.

Enjoy the wonder of feeling expansive and timeless with no boundaries and no limitations. Bask in the freedom, safety, comfort, and bliss of pure beingness.

Mental Pillars

Use what I call Mental Pillars to support your intentions. In construction, pillars are used to strengthen and support walls and roofs. Mental Pillars can be anything that reminds you to connect with a positive feeling or emotion. They help you identify with your desired focus of attention while transforming your thoughts into feelings.

Pillars can be items like a touchstone or crystal, picture, ring, necklace, fond memory, piece of clothing, etc. If you want to feel more love, think of something or someone you love or that reminds you of something/someone you love. Do the same with a desire to feel thankfulness, love, appreciation, forgiveness, gratitude, peace, and wellbeing.

When I am feeling stressed or overwhelmed, I take a few seconds to look at the pictures on my office wall of my family, friends, and pet. Instantly, my feelings transition into love, appreciation, and gratitude. At that moment, I realize how easy it is to transmute the negative into the positive.

When I am feeling anxious or uncomfortable with my surroundings, I touch the souvenir charm on my neck chain that I purchased in Mont Saint Michel, France. I immediately feel the peace and wonder of that magnificent island cathedral. I am transported back to the time of fun and excitement I shared with my wife on that glorious trip.

The mother of an employee I once worked with passed away. My coworker's siblings took their mother's favorite jacket and cut it up into pieces. They made miniature pillows from the jacket pieces and gave each family member one. This was not a sad, sorrowful reminder for them, but a comforting, warm reminder of their mother. It stimulated fond memories and made them feel warm, loved, and appreciated each time they held or looked at the pillow. It reminded them of their mother's love for them.

Occasionally, my wife and I will have a disagreement. I may walk away angry at the moment, but when I look at her mother's picture in my workout room, within seconds I become grateful for her bringing my wife into this world. I feel thankful, grateful, and appreciative. I feel love, peace, and forgiveness.

Discover pillars that work for you. Find something that connects you to the positive memory or experience you wish to feel in that moment. Use Mental Pillars to raise your consciousness to make you feel better about yourself, your situation, and your world.

Meeds

Meeds are fitting rewards which can be used as a fun way to reinforce positivity. Reward yourself for elevating your level of consciousness and changing your mood. Each time you can alter your state of mind by shifting away from a negative mindset, reward yourself.

This reward can be a piece of candy, a nut, sunflower seed, a sticker, or whatever your heart's desire. Each time you reward yourself for steering back on track, you are training yourself to remain in the positive state you prefer.

Back in the 1890s, a Russian physiologist named Ivan Pavlov was researching salivation in dogs in response to being fed. It was a perfect example of classical conditioning which could be utilized in cultivating specific associations between the occurrence of one event and the anticipation of another.

He discovered the dogs responded to various sounds, such as a bell, by salivating in anticipation of being fed. He rang the bell each time just before feeding. When the dogs heard the bell, they salivated. They had become conditioned to the sound of the bell as a prelude to being fed.

Condition yourself to the meed. Once you have rewarded yourself several times for changing your behavior or state of mind with the meed, you will be conditioned to the meeds. In time, just looking at your meed will produce desired results. Give yourself a meed each time you recognize that you have a choice to make and you make the right choice.

The subconscious mind is continuously listening to what the conscious, objective mind tells it. It brings about behavior patterns that are consistent with what the conscious mind says. If we continually think and talk about how we are unhappy with certain situations in our job or family life, then we are reinforcing that reality with the subconscious mind. The subconscious mind will accommodate by pairing your current thoughts with subsequent actions. You move in the direction of your dominant thoughts.

Using meeds helps to create new neural connections that are consistent with your positive intentions. Ring a bell, reward yourself, or do whatever works for you to bring yourself back into alignment with your highest values.

Be SMART

There are acronyms for just about everything. Each teacher has his or her own set regarding various topics. SMART represents my top five, most essential solutions for maintaining the process of personal expansion and development.

S is for Solutions. Unless you can find solutions to your issues, you will continue to remain in your current state. Don't get stuck in your unresolved issues. If you want to expand and evolve into your highest expression, you will need to make use of the tools you have discovered in this book or others you have learned from along the way.

M is for meditate. Numerous scientific studies have shown meditation improves cognitive function, physical wellbeing, and spiritual attunement. Meditation can enhance almost all areas of life. Some of the most brilliant inventions and developmental processes have spawned during people's meditations.

A is for Adapt. It is imperative that you adapt to your environment. We have evolved as a species to our ever-changing world. Throughout millennia, we have adapted to massive changes in our environment, climate, culture, spirituality, business, fitness and health, psychology, technology, and science. If you cannot adapt, you will suffer. When you learn to adapt to your surroundings and experiences, you move forward along the path to an enriched life.

R is for recover. If you fail to recover from adverse events, you may experience unhappiness, strife, ill-health, or a broken spirit. Rapid recovery places you in control. You are not bound by the recurrent thoughts and feelings of past transgressions, catastrophic events, or failures. Recovery is paramount to leading a life free from current or past encumbrances.

T is for tolerant. If you are intolerant of yourself, your behaviors, others, or situations, you may become resentful, bitter, anxious, or deprived. Intolerant people navigate life through a dark cloud. Intolerance breeds contempt and division. Being tolerant provides opportunities to open your heart, free your mind, and expand your consciousness.

Be SMART and listen to your inner guidance system. Follow the leading of spirit and allow life to unfold in a way that is pleasing and uplifting to you. Using your inner guidance is like plugging into an electrical outlet. If you are plugged in and utilizing all the associated benefits, life will expose your highest potential.

Combat Resistance

If you are experiencing doubt or are over-monitoring your decisions and choices, or if you are concerned about how your choices will be received by you or perceived by others, don't resist these feelings. What you resist persists. Refocus and redirect your attention to states of awareness expressed in The Seven Gates (see chapter twenty-two for a refresher).

Consistently bring yourself back into alignment with what you know works best for you. Accept situations as they are, without resistance or judgment. Do not label them as good or bad. Just see them as they are without the adjectives.

Permit yourself to experience your troubling issue fully with all the emotions and physical sensations, then let it go. Ask yourself: "Do I want to remain in this state?", "What purpose is this serving?", or "Who will benefit from this behavior?" Then place your attention back on The Seven Gates. Realize your situation, recover from it, then realign with your highest intentions and refocus in the present moment.

Remember, your current or past issues cannot prevent you from being present in this moment. They have no power over you. You, and you only, can direct your attention and awareness into the present moment where life unfolds for you in the way in which you desire.

"The best day of your life is the one on which you decide your life is your own. No apologies or excuses. No one to lean on, rely on, or blame. The gift of life is yours, it is an amazing journey, and you alone are responsible for the quality of it." —Dan Zadra, businessman, inspirational writer.

From Stressed to Blessed

Try using the "turn-it-on-its-head" Stressed to Blessed Exercise which allows you to reframe your negative situation into one that is more tolerant, acceptant, or bearable. Although it seems counter intuitive, this exercise can reduce pain, stress, anxiety, and frustration by turning up your negative imagining. Use it to adapt to conditions that are out of your control, improve relationships, or handle physical and emotional pain.

Bring yourself into coherence by finding a quiet place where you will not be disturbed for five minutes or so. Start by taking a long, slow, deep breath in and holding it for three seconds before exhaling completely. Twice more, inhale slowly and deeply for another count of three seconds and then exhale completely.

Relax your mind and body, releasing all tension while breathing normally. This brings your mind and body into coherence while slowing your brainwaves into the Alpha state.

Then, bring to mind a current or past troubling personal issue. It may be a failed or strained relationship, physical injury, or a negative emotional issue. Experience the issue wholly and completely. Feel, as real as you can, what it feels like to hold this issue. Next, ask yourself, "What would feel worse than this?" Once you have identified a worse problem, experience that feeling entirely.

Now, imagine another even worse issue. Experience that one fully. Feel the pain, emotional distress, or anxiety—whatever comes up.

Realize exactly what your worse issue is and label it without any negative adjectives.

Recover by relating this worse issue to your current issue. How does it compare?

Realign yourself into coherence by recognizing that your current state is far better than the imagined worse alternatives. Your current situation is not nearly as bad as you thought in comparison. Things could be much worse for you. You can now appreciate your condition and return your attention to the present moment and the affairs at hand.

Refocus on the good things in your life, and on your positive intentions and goals.

Follow this example. Suppose you threw your back out while moving furniture and you are greatly suffering. You have constant, throbbing pain with each movement and with every breath you take.

Now, using the Stressed to Blessed technique, you imagine having a broken back with even more severe pain. That definitely feels worse! Then, you imagine having two broken legs along with the broken back while being immobile and laid up in a hospital.

You *realize* and acknowledge that you have a sore back.

You *recover* by comparing your sore back to your imagined broken back and legs.

You *realign* yourself with the understanding that your sore back is nowhere near the injury of a broken back and legs.

You *refocus* by placing your attention on the present moment and the task at hand.

By following this thought pattern, you have shifted from being stressed to feeling blessed. Now that you understand how much worse things could be for you, a sense of appreciation and gratitude naturally follow along with a reduction in pain.

Once you have completed this short exercise a couple of times, you should be able to do it without the initial breathing relaxation. This exercise can be performed instantly, without hesitation, anytime you are feeling sorry for yourself or are in pain. Just think of what could be worse and be grateful.

You now have many powerful tools to effect change in your life, either maximum or minimum. It's your choice. I challenge you to use as many tools and techniques as it takes to bring happiness, contentment, and excitement into your world.

When you find something that works particularly well for you, keep up with it. Then continue trying other solutions or exercises until you come to the realization that your life now has more meaning and is more satisfying.

Don't worry about what others may think—do what makes you happy! Adopt a positive outlook on life. And remember to share what you have learned with others so they can awaken their potential as well.

Solutions

- Handle interference by taking responsibility for everything. Reframe situations within your mind into those that are conducive to favorable outcomes.

- Seek out the deeper meanings of life. Move from a static mindset into an expansive mindset.

- Use the 4R's. 1. *Realize* your problem and identify with it. 2. *Recover* from it by identifying what could be worse than your problem. 3. *Realign* back into coherency by recognizing that you are better off than the alternative. 4. *Refocus* on your positive intentions and goals in the present moment.

- Create Pillars to support and strengthen your intentions.

- Use Meeds to encourage mood changes, attitudinal shifts, intentions, achievements, and elevated levels of consciousness. Be tenacious!

- Get SMART! Find Solutions to your problems; Meditate habitually; Adapt to your environment; Recover as quickly as possible; Tolerate yourself, your situation, and others.

- Transition from stressed to blessed as often as you can. Perform this exercise whenever you are feeling sorry for yourself, stressed out, in pain, or unhappy.

- Entrain your thoughts and feelings with your higher self and with those around you who are positive.

- Remember, you are never too old or too stuck in your ways to effect change.

Resources

HuffPost Life, The Blog: www.huffpost.com. Search for the article "How to Focus on the Process Instead of the Outcome.

Psychology Today: www.psychologytoday.com.
Search for the article "Reframing, The Transformative
Power of Suffering."

HuffPost Life: www.huffpost.com. Search for the
article "The Importance of Problem-Solving."

WebMD: www.webmd.com. Search for the article "10
Relaxation Techniques That Zap Stress Fast."

**Reminder: You can find all live resource links on
the author's website at AwakenMyPotential.com.**

Closing Thoughts

Shortly after learning to meditate, I began to have dreams at night of flying. During the first couple of years, I would dream I was walking and my feet would suddenly lift from the ground. It was very awkward, and I felt I was not in control. Then, throughout the next several years, I began to float higher and higher.

When I reached a level of about ten to twenty feet above the ground, I became fearful and tried to force myself down. I was afraid to let go and rise to higher elevations. Once I realized that I was holding on to my prior beliefs and comfort levels, however, I began to fly effortlessly.

I could then control my flights with precision, climbing high into the atmosphere over cities, forests, and mountains. I would breeze through cathedrals, tunnels, and incredibly detailed surroundings at will.

Then, I had a dream where I saw a man standing next to his car in a field looking up at me. I swooped down and stretched my hand toward him, offering to bring him along with me. This solidified my intention of helping others learn the techniques and processes that I had discovered.

Everything in this book will not resonate with everyone. Find the suggestions and processes that work best for you and establish ways of implementing them to your benefit.

Find the time to make them happen. Even though you may think you do not have any additional time, you can rearrange your schedule to accommodate what interests you most. Time is subjective. It only exists within your mind.

Fulfill your expectations by adding one or two elements of these processes at a time. Start slowly, so you do not become overwhelmed. Choose the most meaningful or interesting gems and get started immediately.

Once you have experienced positive results, continue on until you have accomplished all of your intentions. Intentions change the world. Intentions lead to mastery. Intentions create excitement, direction, and satisfaction.

I wish for you all of the wonders, thrills, happiness, and contentment life can offer. You are in charge of your destiny. You alone can make a difference in your world.

Expand your knowledge, intuition, and consciousness beyond the threshold. Explore the world of the unknown with the innocent, inquisitive mind of a child. Express yourself with honor, patience, kindness, and love.

Be authentic. Be the real you. Be thankfulness, love, appreciation, forgiveness, gratitude, peace, and wellbeing.

I welcome your comments and reviews. All reviews are extremely important to me and I would really appreciate them. If you prefer, you can email me at dean@awakenmypotential.com with your review.

Before we part, I want to share one last quick story. A friend of mine's ninety-two-year-old mother was preparing to read my first two books and asked me if she was too old at this point in her life to learn new things to awaken her potential. I replied that one is never too old to learn new ways of thinking or being. I want you to know that at any age you can improve your quality of life for your remaining days on this earth.

"Consult not your fears but your hopes and your dreams. Think not about your frustrations, but about your unfulfilled potential. Concern yourself not with what you tried and failed in, but with what it is still possible for you to do." —Pope John XXIII

Other books by Dean Nelson

The Experiential Approach: A Fresh, New Approach for Creating Immediate Personal Power.

The Mindfulness Approach: To Eliminate or Reduce Symptoms of Stress-Related Illnesses.

Visit AwakenMyPotential.com for more information about the author and his books. Read reviews and articles, watch videos, click on links to social media sites, and receive free downloads.

Made in the USA
Middletown, DE
25 June 2021

43164603R00166